GENERATION GAMES

Featuring:

A Certain Term by Michael McManus

&

I F___N' Love You by Charlie Ross Mackenzie

Published by Playdead Press

© Michael McManus 2023

© Charlie Ross Mackenzie 2023

Michael McManus & Charlie Ross Mackenzie have asserted their rights under the Copyright, Design and Patents Act, 1988, to be identified as the authors of their respective works.

A CIP catalogue record for this book is available from the British Library.

ISBN 978-1-915533-13-5

Caution

All rights whatsoever in this play are strictly reserved and application for performance should be sought through the authors before rehearsals begin. No performance may be given unless a license has been obtained.

This book is sold subject to the condition that it shall not by way of trade or otherwise, be lent, resold, hired out, or otherwise circulated without the publisher's prior consent in any form of binding or cover other than that in which it is published and without a similar condition including this condition being imposed on the subsequent purchaser.

Playdead Press
www.playdeadpress.com

This version of this double bill was first performed at the White Bear Theatre, London, on 11th April 2023, in a production lovingly dedicated to the memory of the irrepressible, irreplaceable Paul O'Grady.

CAST & CREATIVES:

A CERTAIN TERM

GRAHAM	**Luke McBride**
JOE	**Simon Stallard**
ROBERT	**Joe Ashman**

Written by **Michael McManus**
Directed by **Bryan Hodgson**

I F___N' LOVE YOU

ADRIAN	**Charlie Ross Mackenzie**
SIMON	**Joe Ashman**

Written by **Charlie Ross Mackenzie**
Directed by **Edward Applewhite**

Lighting Adviser	**Richard Lambert**
Designer	**Philip Normal**
Tech operator / stage manager	**Jaymie Quinn**
Graphic Design	**Nicholas Robinson**

The Plays

A Certain Term

The genesis of this play lies in the research I undertook a decade ago for my book *Tory Pride and Prejudice*, a history of the politics of LGBT+ rights, with a focus on the Conservative party. I was struck then, again and again, by how dramatically the outlooks and first-hand experiences of my interviewees varied, according to their age. There are still the survivors of the pre-1967 generation, who were forced to live their early lives in the shadows; the Gay Pride generation, who took to the streets and made a noise; the first HIV-AIDS generation, which suffered so much ghastly loss; then the Section 28/Stonewall generation; and, now, an entirely new generation, to whom all of that is merely history. I felt at the time this would be perfect material for a play. Now I have written that play.

This double bill was originally scheduled to be staged in March 2020, but fell prey to the pandemic and, specifically, to the first lockdown (of blessed memory). During that dark time, both plays had successful rehearsed performances on Zoom. The past years have changed all our lives and, somehow, this play, which touches (but no longer dwells) upon on an earlier pandemic – the HIV-AIDS pandemic, which unhappily continues to this day in many less favoured parts of the world – simply had to take account of this latest one. For the trial run in 2021 I therefore reinvented the piece, retitled it and entrusted it to a new director and an entirely new team of actors. For this first, full production, there have been (many) more rewrites and we have new actors again. This is not to invalidate, or even to call into question, the considerable work that into previous productions. I must mention, special thanks to Simon Stallard and Luke McGibney for their notable commitment to getting the text right.

Michael McManus

I F___n' Love You

There are those nights, those perfect nights, when the world is put to rights, you look into the soul of the person closest to you and connect with their humanity. Well this isn't one of those! Simon and Adrian are getting ready for a good night's sleep. Trouble is, sleep is difficult when you're prone to overthinking things. As they uncover many things thought forgotten, dealing with fidelity, death, weak bladders and various iterations of Bucks Fizz this will be no easy night's kip. OK, well maybe it is one of those nights!

When I was a stand-up comedian, I was often asked, "Where do you get your material from?" As a writer it's, "Where do you get your ideas from?". For this one, it truly came to me in a dream. So, there I was, at 2.37am, one night in July 2019, furiously typing away to get those first few lines of dialogue down. I subsequently took out the talking gorilla, of course. The rest fell into place over the next few months. It's very exciting to be presenting it to you here, in a full production for the first time, at the fabulous White Bear Theatre. I really hope you enjoy it. And if you really feel it needs a talking gorilla, let me know and I may put it back in!

Charlie Ross Mackenzie

Biographies

Michael McManus | Writer, *A Certain Term*

Michael is author and/or editor of a number of books, including *Tory Pride and Prejudice* (Biteback, 2011); and *Edward Heath: A Singular Life* (Elliott & Thompson, 2016), which was "Book of the Week" in the *Daily Mail*. This is his third play. His first, *An Honourable Man*, had two successful runs in 2018 here at the White Bear, and was published by Playdead Press. His second, *Maggie & Ted*, began life as a radio-style production at the White Bear in 2019 and has since appeared at the Garrick Theatre and the Yvonne Arnaud Theatre in Guildford. A substantially rewritten, fully-staged production of *Maggie & Ted* will tour the UK in 2024, as will a brand-new political comedy, commissioned by the Yvonne Arnaud.

As an actor, he has most recently featured in two plays in the Scenesaver *Just Write!* Festival (White Bear Theatre). He played the Marquess de Lancy in the 150th anniversary revival of Mrs. Inchbold's *Animal Magnetism* (Knebworth House) with the original production having featured, and been stage-managed by Charles Dickens. Michael created the roles of Sir James Mitchell in *Direct Action* by Githa Sowerby (directed online by Graham Watts) and Sir Donald Wolfit in *The Trial of Donald Wolfit* (White Bear Theatre). He also took on various roles in the *Hog in the Limelight* lockdown series, including Joe Newman in *To Walk With Kings;* The Reverend Cyril Starr in Glenn Chandler's *Lord Dismiss Us;* and Alderman Roberts (plus Denis Healey, Tony Benn, Roy Jenkins et al.) in *Maggie & Ted*.

**Charlie Ross Mackenzie | Writer,
I F___n' Love You / Adrian**
Charlie is a celebrated comedian, writer and broadcaster.

He has written and performed a number of highly praised shows, which have been performed at the Edinburgh International Fringe Festival and on tour. He has frequently presented programmes for BBC Radio Scotland, including co-presenting the award-winning *Macaulay And Co.* with broadcasting legend Fred MacAulay. His book *Smiles and Tribulations: A Comedian's Tale* was published in 2010. He has also written for BBC TV's *River City*. Charlie is also the creator and co-host of the podcast *Victim to Heartstopper*, which looks at the world of LGBT+ TV and film.

Together with musical director Matt Malone and Bryan Hodgson, Michael and Charlie have also been working together on a new musical featuring the songs of Marc Almond and Soft Cell, which had a successful showcase at The Vaults in London, in October 2018 (as *Tainted – A New Musical*, produced by Michael McManus) and is currently going into pre-production.

Joe Ashman | Robert (A Certain Term) / Simon (I F___n' Love You)
After working in the West End as a child, Joe trained at Tring Park and, after graduating in 2012, he worked in the West End again on musicals *Our House* and *Rent*. In 2017, Joe landed a role in the Netflix Original Series *Free Rein*. He

spent two years on this show, which won 2 Emmy awards. Joe then moved onto the BBC & Netflix collaboration project *Get Even*. Most recently, Joe played William in BBC's *Casualty*.

Luke McGibney | Graham (*A Certain Term*)

Classically trained, Luke received a scholarship at The Oxford School of Drama.

His professional debut was at The Royal Court playing Andrew, a prison instructor in *The Barred*.

He has recently completed playing the Creature in *Frankenstein* (The Hawth Theatre). He has also toured extensively throughout Australia, playing Basil Fawlty at Sydney Opera House. Other theatre credits include comedy *Smash* (Oxford Playhouse), *The Barred* (Theatre 503), *Selling the Sky* (Yorkshire Playhouse) and Irish play *Body and Blood* (The Kings Head).

His film and television work includes Netflix *The Intent and Containment*. He also played Fred Perry's father in Channel 4's *Rise*. He has been nominated by the Midlands Royal Television Society for Best Actor, for his work in the award-winning British indie film *Remora*, in which he played the antagonist Eric Mann, a seaside resort gangster.

Outside acting Luke is a stand-up comedian, improviser and writer, currently working on *Frankenprov*, a Gothic, improvised show for next year.

Simon Stallard | Joe (*A Certain Term*)

Simon trained at the Guildford School of Acting, graduating in 2015. He has been nominated in the Off West End Awards for Best Male Performance (*Kes*, 2018) and Best Male in a Supporting Role (*Different From the Others*, 2019). He is also a musician and Musical Director of touring company This Is My Theatre.

Theatre credits include: *Frankenstein, The Poppy Red, Treasure Island* (The Hawth Theatre); *An Eton Mess* (Reading at the Vaudeville Theatre); *The Railway Children, Pride & Prejudice, Jane Eyre, The Three Musketeers, The Wind in the Willows* (TIMT); *Maggie & Ted* (The Yvonne Arnaud); *The Trial of Donald Wolfit, Different From The Others, A Little Hero* (White Bear Theatre); *Ciphers* (Phoenix Arts Centre); *Kes* (The Jack Studio Theatre); *Tainted: A New Musical* (The Vaults Waterloo); *Blue Stockings* (The Cockpit Theatre); *Taking an Age, The Calm* (Who Said Theatre); *The Bridge* (The London Theatre); *Table* (Waterloo East Theatre); *The Broken Heart* (Wanamaker Festival, Shakespeare's Globe); *Night Horses* (La Chapelle Gely, Montpellier); *The Radicalisation of Bradley Manning* (The Ivy Arts Centre).

Edward Applewhite | Director (*I F___n' Love You*)

Edward Applewhite trained at Guildford School of Acting and worked as an actor in TV and theatre before being appointed artistic director of Wigan Pier Theatre Company and subsequently founding Wigan Pier Youth Theatre. As a writer, he was commissioned to write a musical adaptation of Dickens' *A Christmas Carol*, won a tourist award for a Murder

Mystery weekend and wrote Lancashire's contribution to Our Town celebrations in the Millennium Dome.

He is currently the Head of Drama and Director of the Acting Course at Tring Park School for the Performing Arts, directing over 50 productions. More recently he has also returned to performing, playing the Dame at Marina Sands Theatre in Singapore and the 'beardy weirdo' Dave in the independent feature film *Incidental Characters*. He is currently writing a radio comedy drama.

Bryan Hodgson | Director (*A Certain Term*)

Bryan is a writer and director and trained at GSA, graduating in 2014. His directing credits include: *Beauty and the Beast* (Wyvern Theatre), *Elf The Musical, Spider's Web* (PPA), *Alright Bitches, Tommy On Top* (Above the Stag Theatre), *Murder for Two* (The Barn Theatre), *Merrily We Roll Along* (Trinity Laban), *The Tailor-Made Man, Gay Generations* (White Bear Theatre), *The Great Pause* (Pluck Productions), *Jack and the Blingstalk* (Harold Pinter Theatre), *Elegies for Angels, Punks & Raging Queens, Twang!! The Musical* (Union Theatre), *Teechers* (New Wimbledon Theatre Studio), *The Importance of Being Earnest* (The Barn Theatre & The Turbine Theatre), *Tainted* (The Vaults), *Salad Days* (Union Theatre, Bath Theatre Royal, & UK Tour), *Kray Kray* (Theatre N16), *Waiting Room* – Workshop (Upstairs at the Gatehouse), *Cymbeline* (The Space, London), *The Fellowship* (Hen and Chickens Theatre & Yvonne Arnaud Theatre), *Wind in the Willows, Dorothy* (Waterloo East Theatre).

As Associate Director; *Moby Dick The Musical* (Union Theatre).

As Assistant Director; *Judy!* (The Arts Theatre), *Rent* (Pleasance Theatre), *Casa Valentina* (Southwark Playhouse).

Bryan has written several plays, all of which have been professionally produced around the UK; *The Wind in the Willows*, *The Fellowship*, *Kray Kray*, *The Road to Oz* and *King Kong (ish)*.

Philip Normal | Designer

Philip Normal is an artist and designer based in South-East London, with a shop in Brixton. He has designed costumes for the legendary "anti-drag" performer David Hoyle at Soho Theatre. https://philipnormal.shop

The White Bear Theatre

The **White Bear Theatre** was founded in 1988 and focuses on new writing and lost classics. It exists to nurture and develop exceptional new and existing talent and offer a space where risks can be taken.

Notable artists who have cut their teeth at The White Bear Theatre include: Joe Penhall, Emily Watson, Mehmet Ergen, Tamzin Outhwaite, Kwame Kwei-Armah, Vicky Featherstone, Torben Betts, and Lucinda Coxon. The White Bear Theatre has also developed and hosted work by a new generation of theatre makers including Verity Bargate Winner Vicky Jones, Blanche McIntyre, The Ugly Sisters and Simon Evans. Former White Bear Theatre Associates include Adam Spreadbury-Maher and Box of Tricks Theatre. Founder and Artistic director Michael Kingsbury is on the board of The Society Of Independent Theatres, which represents leading Off West-End theatres including the Finborough, Theatre 503, Park Theatre and the New Diorama.

White Bear Theatre
138 Kennington Park Road
London
SE11 4DJ

www.whitebeartheatre.co.uk

Thanks to:

Michael Kingsbury and Team White Bear

Elliot Robinson at Playdead Press

Lewis Chandler

Daniel Cornish

Matthew Darling

Dickon Farmar

Brandon Gale

David & Paddy Hunt

Oliver McFadden

Diane McHale

James King

James Lavender

Ed O'Connor

Stephen Omer

Francesca Padovani

Michael Prescott

Nicholas Robinson

Robert Sladden

Peter Tatchell

For Peter Tatchell, Michael Cashman, Ian McKellen and everyone else who spoke out when too many others were silent.
Michael

For all my friends and family who put up with me on this mad showbiz journey, thank you.

Dedicated to my dear sister Katherine.
Charlie

A CERTAIN TERM

by Michael McManus

SCENE 1 – JOE

Saturday 11 November 2023, late afternoon. GRAHAM's flat. GRAHAM is preparing busily for a party, looking at his watch. Half dressed, no trousers, he wears black socks, polished shoes, pants, kimono and bow tie under an apron. A buzzer goes. Once, twice, insistently. GRAHAM looks at the clock.

GRAHAM: What? (He answers the buzzer). Hello?

JOE: Hey. It's Joe.

GRAHAM: (*Away from the mic*) Joe? (*To the mic*) If it's a delivery, just leave it in the hallway. Thanks. (*Buzzer goes again*) Yes?

JOE: I'm not a delivery driver.

GRAHAM: (*Away from the mic*) He's not a delivery driver. (*To the mic*) You're not a Jehovah's Witness?

JOE: It's Joe. I'm here for the party.

GRAHAM: Party? There is no party.

JOE: You invited me, the other night.

GRAHAM: (*Away from the mic*) I need to stop drinking. (*To the mic*) Yes, of course I did. So sorry, please come on up. I'll buzz you in. (*Now to himself*) Oh no.

He has suddenly remembered he's not properly dressed. He dashes to get changed. Too late. His front door is not locked. He changes direction, to lock it.

JOE: Coo ee! (*JOE sticks his head around the door*) Hello.

GRAHAM: Hello.

JOE: Hello.

GRAHAM: Hello.

JOE is clutching a carrier bag.

JOE: Are we having the party out here?

GRAHAM: Sorry, please come in. It's been one of those days. You know, hostess with the mostest. No, you probably don't. (*Enter JOE. GRAHAM keeps his front to JOE, to avoid accidental exposure*) I'm just getting ready.

JOE: Great, looks lovely.

GRAHAM: Well, thank you for coming. What a surprise.

JOE: You don't remember me, do you?

GRAHAM: How could I forget you? Joe. Joe Joe. Joe Cool, Joe the Man /

JOE: Oh God, this is embarrassing.

GRAHAM: No, no, please. Joe from the other night.

JOE: And?

GRAHAM: We were drinking... clearly. And we did, did a lot of drinking... and... did we... you and I, you know?

JOE: No.

GRAHAM: Of course we didn't.

JOE: So where do I get changed?

GRAHAM: What?

JOE: That's why I came early. You asked me to bring my hot pants.

GRAHAM: I did?

JOE: No. I'm yanking your chain.

GRAHAM: Christ, you nearly gave me a heart attack. I deserved that.

JOE: So. Party?

GRAHAM: Look, the thing is, I don't think it's your cup of tea. It's going to be a room full of old farts like me.

JOE: I wouldn't have come if you were an old fart.

GRAHAM: That's very kind of you, but trust me, I've got one foot in the grave.

JOE: I could help you prepare? I'd look great in a maid's outfit.

GRAHAM: Really? You're sure? Well, that changes things a little, but why not. We've got 45 minutes… and… 30 seconds to be precise. I think I ought to put on some trousers, don't you?

JOE: Yeah, might be a good idea.

GRAHAM: Please, sit. Not that side, sorry. Sorry. Here. Not there. (*GRAHAM now exits into the bedroom and continues the conversation. JOE looks around*)

JOE: Nice place, very retro.

GRAHAM: You mean old?

JOE: You've got a thing about "old". No, I mean retro. Very cool.

GRAHAM: I must be retro then.

JOE: Tell me more about this old farts party.

GRAHAM: Just old cronies really. I've known most of them since you were in short trousers.

JOE: Sounds amazing.

GRAHAM: It's an elephants' graveyard.

JOE: So much history.

GRAHAM: Excuse me, I'm not that old.

JOE: I mean living history.

GRAHAM: Nice recovery.

JOE: Thank you.

GRAHAM: We convene annually. Apart from 2020 and 2021, of course.

JOE: The lockdown years.

GRAHAM: Except for that bumbling fat oaf, Johnson.

JOE: BoJo?

GRAHAM: I wish he'd eaten a batshit sandwich and died.

JOE: Harsh.

GRAHAM: Not as harsh as last year.

JOE: Oh?

GRAHAM: West Ham lost in the afternoon.

JOE: Nothing unusual in that.

GRAHAM returns.

GRAHAM: You're a fellow sufferer? A Hammer?

JOE: Oh God, no. It's just… West Ham.

GRAHAM: Bitch. (*The trousers*). Too bright?

JOE: Too bright.

GRAHAM: (*He walks back into the bedroom to try again*) We drink, we reminisce, then we drink some more. Usually I put on "I Will Survive", someone starts puking and someone else starts crying. Last year someone micturated over the pot plant.

JOE looks at the rather sad pot plant.

JOE: Micturated?

GRAHAM: Have a pee pee. Squeeze the lizard. Strain the vegetables.

JOE: Got it. Thanks.

JOE looks at the sad plant in a new light.

GRAHAM: It's a cross-section of our oldest friends.

JOE: "Our"?

GRAHAM returns.

GRAHAM: "My". Yes, my friends. (*GRAHAM looks at the framed photo of ROBERT*). Better?

GRAHAM indicates his trousers.

JOE: Much better. It sounds very interesting.

GRAHAM: Interesting? No one finds me interesting.

JOE: I do. I brought wine. Mateus Rosé.

GRAHAM: (*Laughing*) Mateus Rosé?

JOE: Apparently it was very popular in –

GRAHAM: In the Middle Ages?

JOE: Bit naff?

GRAHAM: Look, why don't you just /

JOE: Leave /

GRAHAM: No. I was going to say, you might as well, have a drink.

JOE: Oh. Can I get a white wine?

GRAHAM: Get one?

JOE: Get one. Ta.

GRAHAM: Get one? Or have one?

JOE: Whatever.

GRAHAM: Good God, I feel like I'm trying to share a sophisticated mode of communication with a Brexiteer.

JOE: I'm so, so sorry. My dear chap, would it inconvenience you ever so much, if I was to /

GRAHAM: Were to – classic subjunctive /

JOE: Have a glass of white wine off of you?

GRAHAM: Off of you? From me. Of course. My pleasure.

JOE: Do you always talk like this?

GRAHAM: Well excuse me for honouring the Queen's English.

JOE: Surely the King's English?

GRAHAM: Oh God, yes. What a depressing thought. First the Government was run by the reserve team, now it's the Royal Family.

GRAHAM opens the first bottle of the night and pours. He hands a huge glass of white wine to JOE.

JOE: What's the toast?

GRAHAM: To reserve teams.

JOE: To reserve teams.

SCENE 2 – GRAHAM

GRAHAM carries on doing things. It's all intricately scheduled, to the nearest minute.

JOE: So.

GRAHAM: So.

JOE: No, you, please /

GRAHAM: Please, after you /

JOE: So, you're a writer.

GRAHAM: Oh yes. There they are. My "children".

JOE: That's so cool.

GRAHAM: I work to live, and I write to… You know, I don't know why I write. The total royalties there wouldn't even finance the bracket, let alone the IKEA shelf that they so ostentatiously adorn.

JOE: Maybe it's a calling? Along with acting?

GRAHAM: How'd you know about that?

JOE: I've seen you.

GRAHAM: No one has seen me. Nowadays all I do is fringe, usually above some pretentious, over-priced pub.

JOE: Isn't that where all the best, new stuff is going on?

GRAHAM: It demands infinite steadfastness, commitment and talent. But pays bugger-all money. So. Was I good? Really. Be honest. Say it, how it is. No pressure. Really. Mmm.

JOE: It was, um, well, it was um /

GRAHAM: It was um? Nice review.

JOE: It was about a kind of... tree.

GRAHAM: Ah! "Bough Down". What a piece. Charting the slow, un-regarded decline of a mortally injured apple tree. "Bough... Down". (*GRAHAM bows, very OTT*). A tree as metaphor for man's heartless indifference to /

JOE: Yeah, that. That one.

GRAHAM: So? What did you think?

JOE: Oh, it was, you were –

GRAHAM: Oh! it was –

JOE: Oh... er... er... you were... I think... er... Oh! A pantomime! You've written a pantomime? That is so cool.

GRAHAM: Yes, well, kindly give it back.

JOE playfully refuses. He opens the script.

JOE: Oh no I won't.

GRAHAM: Oh yes you bloody will. Hand it over.

JOE: And this'll be performed?

GRAHAM: We start rehearsing in ten days' time.

JOE: London Palladium?

GRAHAM: Not exactly.

JOE: So? Where can I see your masterpiece performed?

GRAHAM: Frinton-on-Sea and Wivenhoe. Senior Amateur Dramatics. God's waiting room on a stage.

JOE: (*Reads from the script*) "I'm taking my band to South Korea".

GRAHAM: Seoul?

JOE: No. Rock and Roll. (*GRAHAM desperately seeks approbation*) That's terrible. "What's that aftershave you're wearing?".

GRAHAM: It's called "Come to Me".

JOE: "Doesn't smell like come to me!" Will you get away with this?

GRAHAM: I don't know and I don't really care. The next one, the next one. It's the best.

JOE: "I went to a dreadful concert in Malaysia".

GRAHAM: Singapore?

JOE: "The entire band was terrible".

GRAHAM: Singapore. Singer poor.

JOE: That's dreadful.

GRAHAM: Everyone's a critic. Right, napkin time. (*Exit GRAHAM*) Have a nose around. Don't be too nosey.

JOE: Have you always lived alone?

GRAHAM: Oh no. I did have a partner. For a time. In my salad days. (*He re-enters and puts napkins onto a table*) When I was green in judgement.

JOE: What happened?

GRAHAM: The call of the wild was too strong for him.

JOE: Sorry if I. So, which is your favourite? From your books I mean.

GRAHAM: My history of gay rights.

JOE: Oh. Just gay rights?

GRAHAM: That's enough for one book. It was remaindered years ago. And they pulped the left-over copies without telling me. Bastards. (*He hands the book to JOE*). A year of my life went into that.

JOE: Amazing.

GRAHAM: You haven't opened it yet.

JOE: Writing a book is amazing. How many people get to do that? "Prejudice and Pride" by... I thought your name was Graham?

GRAHAM: What's in a name? I think a *nom de plume* allows books to have their own lives.

JOE: Really?

GRAHAM: I'm not like other people.

JOE: You should be proud.

GRAHAM: Right. Time for the Pringles.

As GRAHAM exits, JOE kicks off his shoes. He is wearing rainbow socks. GRAHAM returns, looks at JOE's socks and shakes his head.

JOE: What? The socks?

GRAHAM: Your life is just so different from how mine was/

JOE: Because of my socks?

GRAHAM: When I was growing up, I'd see straight couples everywhere, kissing and cuddling and gazing adoringly at each other/

JOE: Whereas, if you did anything similar with someone you loved/

GRAHAM: My God, stop. Show the slightest tittle of affection in public and game over/

JOE: Tittle?

GRAHAM: Yes, tittle.

JOE: Like a little tit?

GRAHAM: This is like wading through treacle. Look, let me tell you, when I was sixteen, I confided in my GP, that I thought I might be queer.

JOE: You thought?

GRAHAM: She asked me, "What makes you feel aroused? The thought of male genitalia, or a pair of mammaries" /

JOE: Mammaries?

GRAHAM: Mammaries! That's what passed for sympathetic and helpful guidance, in the 1990s.

JOE: What did you say?

GRAHAM: End of conversation. I knew what the answer was, but I wasn't going to say it out loud. My life was blighted from the off. And you don't get a second go.

JOE: At least you're not one of those resentful, bitter old queens /

GRAHAM: Easy, tiger, don't say anything we might both live to regret /

JOE: As if /

GRAHAM: I may be acquainted with one or two, well-worn gay tropes /

JOE: The ones who spent their best years pretending to be totally asexual /

GRAHAM: Pretty much the only ones who came out in my day /

JOE: "In my day" /

GRAHAM: Cheeky sod.

JOE: I just meant, you aren't that old/

GRAHAM: Bless. The only ones who came out "when I were a lad" were the pink, camp powder puffs whom everyone could spot a mile off anyway. Whilst I was "one of those", I was emphatically not one of those.

JOE: Very much not.

GRAHAM: By "playing it straight", I could retain all my privileges.

JOE: I had a girlfriend once. When I was seventeen.

GRAHAM: Good God. How awful for you.

JOE: No, she was alright. It just wasn't right for me.

GRAHAM: Oooh, so you are a fully-fledged, fellow fairy?

JOE: That is such an outmoded, heteronormative, artificial societal construct.

GRAHAM: That's me told.

JOE: Those definitions are redundant now.

GRAHAM: Didn't we meet in a gay bar?

JOE: How can a bar be gay? It's an inanimate object. Unless you mean "gay" as in "that's so gay", as in, it's rubbish.

GRAHAM: Excuse me, gay is not rubbish.

JOE: I know. Definitions, I don't know, they limit. They confine. They isolate. It's just a bar. A fun bar where everyone can feel comfortable and safe. *"The Gutter Hearts, where everyone can be themself"*.

GRAHAM: "Themself"?

JOE: Themself.

GRAHAM: That's not even a word.

JOE: It is now.

GRAHAM: Henceforth I shall make a point of boycotting the place, for offences against the King's English.

JOE: If you'd done that, you may never have met me.

GRAHAM: Might never have met me. Oh, never mind, I sense this gambolling, syntactically challenged, lost sheep is loathe to return to the cold comfort of orderly syntax.

JOE: Pompous sod.

GRAHAM: I am not pompous.

JOE: You so are, but it's fine.

GRAHAM: I see the admiration in your eyes.

JOE: "Themself" is gender neutral.

GRAHAM: "Themself" is bollocks. An aberration.

JOE: I like ABBA.

GRAHAM: So do I. So good.

JOE: I'm just saying – new concepts, new ways of living – new words.

GRAHAM: Thinking that way is your luxury.

JOE: It's a different world now. We can show affection. Be vulnerable. Boy in a dress, girl in a dinner suit. And the other way around. And everything in between.

GRAHAM: Christ, we had our heads kicked in, if our ties were too colourful or our trousers were too tight.

JOE: Assuming you were wearing any.

GRAHAM: Touché. So how was coming out for you? If that's even a thing any more?

JOE: OK, I suppose. A few tears, a bit of blame game. Then "Strictly" came on and calm was restored.

GRAHAM: Jesus. We really do have nothing in common.

JOE: What about you?

GRAHAM: Ah, well now. When I did face facts…

JOE: "Face facts"?

GRAHAM: First I had to dig deep, in search of the real me, on the off chance he'd somehow survived, buried away, deep down inside.

JOE: This was when?

GRAHAM: 2000.

JOE: How old were you then?

GRAHAM: 23 September.

JOE: It's getting very exact.

GRAHAM: A Saturday.

JOE: Of course.

GRAHAM: At around 10.47pm.

JOE: Now you're scaring me. Did you tell your parents?

GRAHAM: No. I left it too late.

JOE: I'm sorry.

GRAHAM: I imagine they were happier, not knowing.

JOE: Why did you leave it so… I mean, you must have been, like, twenty?

GRAHAM: I wasn't like twenty. I was twenty.

JOE: Oooh. Excuse me.

GRAHAM: The first same-sex kiss on TV was a sweet, domestic peck on the forehead. Even at the tender age of eight, somehow, I knew it was important. "East Benders", thundered the tabloids.

JOE: At least the BBC did broadcast it /

GRAHAM: Thereafter, every queer character had to be a temperamental and borderline psychotic, histrionic and utterly miserable... person. Some bloody role models.

JOE: Well, at least that's changed.

GRAHAM: Has it?

JOE: Fair point.

GRAHAM: (*Partly as Thatcher*) "Children are told they have an inalienable right to be gay". And they cheered the heartless cow. Half of them were queers. Tory bastards.

JOE: Hey, I vote Tory.

GRAHAM: Excuse me?

JOE: Joke. Obviously.

GRAHAM: You little cock muffin.

JOE: Little?

GRAHAM: Alright. "Cock muffin". You don't, do you?

JOE: No! And children must have the right to be gay. To be whatever they want.

GRAHAM: For her it was "a choice".

JOE: The only "choice" is to be nice, or not be nice. Stupid muppets.

GRAHAM: Yes, stupid muppets.

JOE: Why'd they do it?

GRAHAM: (*Pointing*) Read the book.

JOE: Thought it was out of print?

GRAHAM: I'll lend you a precious copy. Maybe. Fine. Story time. In the 80s, the gays became political pawns, buffeted between "loony left" and radical right – a perfect storm. A perfect shit storm.

JOE: And people went along with it because /

GRAHAM: Because they were scared. In less than two decades, gay sex went from being illegal, to readily available, to potentially fatal. Social pariahs once more.

JOE: I can imagine.

GRAHAM: You can imagine, living in fear of a plague?

JOE: COVID. Duh.

GRAHAM: Not the same.

JOE: Look, I do know –

GRAHAM: And a certain term suddenly arrived on the scene: "Faggot". Uch.

JOE: And no one stood up for you?

GRAHAM: No. Except for Princess Di, when she did her laying on of hands.

JOE: Things are better now.

GRAHAM: Oh yes. For now. Personally I'm waiting for the next load of turds to float down the river and take our rights away, all over again.

JOE: Lighten up. Party. Pringle?

GRAHAM: You didn't live through the 80s.

JOE: I didn't have to.

GRAHAM: We who remain, must never forget. But then, if you don't much value life, why fear death?

JOE: Drama Queen.

GRAHAM: I'll let that go.

JOE: Why thank you, sir.

GRAHAM: It's not dying young that's an offence against nature for a gay man, you know. It's growing old. We become invisible.

JOE: I see you.

GRAHAM: I was adored once, you know, by a devoted, female admirer /

JOE: Oooh /

GRAHAM: In sixth form. Pursued by the girl everyone desired. Libby Jones. She's a hot-shot lawyer now. Oh, she was the pick of the litter alright. If only I'd wanted it. We chatted and held hands and kissed and had a meal or two, then she tried to seduce me.

JOE: Amazing. As in "amazing". Not "amazing".

GRAHAM: The distinction being?

JOE: I didn't mean anything by it. You're very pendantic.

GRAHAM: It's pedantic /

JOE: I know. It's a meta joke. So, this "physical event" with Libby?

GRAHAM: Oh no, no, no, I couldn't. Heave at the very thought.

JOE: You are so sad.

GRAHAM: Yes, I suppose I am, a little.

JOE: You're also funny.

GRAHAM: (*Partly in Australian Accent*) I have my moments. *"I don't know whether they built that great wall of suburbia to keep us in, or to keep them out, but the city is the safest place for us"*. Priscilla, Queen of the Desert. (*JOE applauds*) I thank you.

JOE: We're really getting each other into the party mood, aren't we?

GRAHAM: It's not a normal party.

JOE: Well of course not. It's a gay old party.

GRAHAM: That's enough of the "old", thank you very much /

JOE: I'm saying "gay" though. Your favourite label.

GRAHAM: Right, time to fetch the component parts of my legendary *pièce de résistance*.

GRAHAM exits.

JOE: It all sounds *fantabulosa*.

GRAHAM: I do hope so. Though we shall be another man down.

JOE: How so?

GRAHAM: Trevor. He survived queer-bashings, losing his job as a teacher, AIDS, all that, then died of COVID. Bit of a cough one day, dead the next.

JOE: Oh. Sorry. That's terrible. (*Beat*) Good turn-out otherwise?

GRAHAM: Ha! Half of them are actors. They'll go anywhere for free food. (*GRAHAM re-enters the room*). I see you found the record collection.

JOE: Always the first thing to check out, right?

GRAHAM: Now vinyl, that is retro.

JOE: Put something on. Something that means a lot to you.

GRAHAM: Really?

JOE: Really.

GRAHAM: OK. (*He puts on some music*) Sorry, it doesn't feel terribly appropriate.

JOE: Maybe you need a boyfriend.

GRAHAM: Trust me, I've tried. (*Turns off the music*) Sadly my aftershave appears to contain a powerful man deterrent.

JOE: There's someone for everyone, they say.

GRAHAM: There was. But not any more.

JOE: More fish in the sea. You know.

GRAHAM: I don't think so. My ocean of possibility ran dry many, many moons ago. Oh, but aren't I the garrulous one? Tell me everything about you.

JOE: It's difficult to know where to start /

GRAHAM: I don't believe it! Aaaaargh!

JOE: Oh cheers.

GRAHAM: The wine. Of all the things to forget.

JOE: What?

GRAHAM: Oregon Pinot Noir.

JOE: And you told me off for not speaking English?

GRAHAM: It's a wine. A red wine.

JOE: Oh. Like that posh French one /

GRAHAM: Don't you dare say it /

JOE: Chateauneuf du Pape. (*GRAHAM flinches, very theatrically*). You are such a snob.

GRAHAM: Why, thank you. Oh, biscuit barrels. I even bought half a case in specially /

JOE: What happened?

GRAHAM: I drank it. I absolutely promised Julian/

JOE: Julian.

GRAHAM: It's embarrassing.

JOE: Being called Julian?

GRAHAM: No, you callow fool, the wine. It's a gay status symbol thing. A talking point. If I don't whip it out at the vital moment, I'll never hear the end of it.

JOE: All about the show.

GRAHAM: Yes, darling, yes, of course it is.

JOE: I'll pop out and get some for you.

GRAHAM: You don't "just pop out and get" Oregon Pinot Noir.

JOE: Pardon me.

GRAHAM: It's as common as the Holy Grail. I'll have to go to my dealer /

JOE: Ooooh, dealer /

GRAHAM: Not that kind of dealer. It's a 20-minute round trip.

JOE: I'll come with you. Our first road trip. You can be Louise.

GRAHAM: Not this time, Thelma.

JOE: A shared cultural reference.

GRAHAM: No, you'd best stay here, in case I get stuck in traffic. If anyone comes early, tell them you're the new house boy. Buggeration. You'll have to do the hedgehog.

JOE: Do the hedgehog?

JOE tries a strange dance ("the hedgehog")

GRAHAM: It's always the last thing I do. Otherwise the cheese gets soggy and the pineapple chunks dry out.

GRAHAM goes to the kitchen and produces the basis of the hedgehog – half a grapefruit, wrapped in metal foil, together with a tray of cheese blocks and pineapple chunks.

On me. Quick. This is the hedgehog's face. Then each spike is like this. Not too deep. Like this. Like this.

GRAHAM demonstrates how to do the hedgehog. JOE is giggling.

JOE: OK, OK, I'll do the hedgehog.

GRAHAM: Try to use them all up.

JOE: Alright Nigella, I've got it. Go fetch your gay status symbol talking point.

GRAHAM: Don't do anything I wouldn't do.

JOE: That leaves me plenty of room for manoeuvre.

GRAHAM: Great, bye!

GRAHAM exits, leaving the door open. JOE grimly contemplates the nascent hedgehog, then samples the punch and gasps for breath at the strength and horror of it.

SCENE 3 – ROBERT

ROBERT: Sorry. The door was open.

JOE: Fuck me. I was... er... doing the hedgehog.

ROBERT: Robert. That normally elicits a response.

JOE: Joseph. My friends call me Joe. Some friends of mine had a dog called Robert.

ROBERT: Really? How... quaintly canine. Pleased to meet you, Joseph.

JOE: You here for the party? Graham had to pop out /

ROBERT: He forgot something?

JOE: He forgot something.

ROBERT: Typical.

JOE: Some fancy wine. Organ Peeny Wah?

ROBERT: Sounds like a dodgy porn star.

JOE: As opposed to a respectable porn star?

ROBERT: Fair point.

JOE: (*OTT US Accent*) Organ Peeny Wah really chews some dick. Sorry.

ROBERT: Don't be, don't be. Ham always was a bit pretentious.

JOE: Ham?

ROBERT: Do you mind if I /

JOE: Oh sorry, yes. Of course. Come in, come in. Sorry. Please, sit down. Can I get you anything?

ROBERT fully enters the space.

ROBERT: Not just at the moment, but thank you. And do stop saying sorry.

JOE: Sorry.

ROBERT: So how do you know Graham?

JOE: How well, or just how?

ROBERT: Either. Both?

JOE: We met last week.

ROBERT: And where was that, I wonder? Did he take you up the Shard?

JOE: No. We met last week, in a bar.

ROBERT: Not very original.

JOE: Serves a purpose.

ROBERT: A gay bar?

JOE: I don't believe in gay bars.

ROBERT: You don't believe in fairies in the garden of your bottom?

JOE: I don't like… labels.

ROBERT: You seem a bit young to be one of Ham's parties.

JOE: I could say the same about you. Not what I was expecting. But Graham did invite me. He was pissed and invited me to the party. And he forgot.

ROBERT: So Ham has a <u>stalker</u>?

JOE: How do you know him?

ROBERT: How do you know I know him?

JOE: Stop being weird. You obviously know him.

ROBERT: I discovered him in a play. Hence "Ham".

JOE: Harsh.

ROBERT: Have you seen him act?

JOE: Well, yes. You know. He was playing a kind of a… talking tree.

ROBERT: Was he wooden?

JOE: That's terrible. So was the play.

ROBERT: He does know how to pick them.

JOE: His bark was worse than his bite. Oh. Ham. Ham as in "ham" Gray-Ham? It's a double pun! I like it.

ROBERT: Top of the class.

JOE: That's really funny. So, where did you "discover" him?

ROBERT: In a dirty old attic, above a Soho boozer.

JOE: Ohh.

ROBERT: No, it was a pub theatre.

JOE: Ah. Same as me.

ROBERT: A common thread at last. Sleazy, filthy, degenerate, like most pub theatre.

JOE: Nice.

ROBERT: Sticky walls. Sticky carpets. Sticky everything/

JOE: COVID shut these places down for a year and they still didn't find time to clean the floors.

ROBERT: The play was a bit crappy. <u>Really</u> crappy. "Experimental" they called it. Too political. Angry. Grrrrrangry.

JOE: Yawn.

ROBERT: Ten minutes in, I was dearly wishing I'd never turned up. Then "it" happened.

JOE: Do tell.

ROBERT: Suddenly, Ham was talking at me. And I mean right at me.

JOE: Why you?

ROBERT: Perhaps he sensed I was dozing off, I don't know. He started on at me /

JOE: What about?

ROBERT: Berating me, all about the miners /

JOE: Children or coal?

ROBERT: Coal.

JOE: Oh yeah.

ROBERT: He hectored me, all about how people like me had been complicit in the Tories destroying their jobs, families and communities.

JOE: Sounds ghastly.

ROBERT: It was. I didn't know how to respond. Or whether I should respond.

JOE: Did you?

ROBERT: No, I kept schtumm, but I damn nearly told him to get stuffed.

JOE: You should have. I would.

ROBERT: I was transfixed. After the show, I waited for him in the bar. He apologised for starting on at me. I told him there was no need. Then I just sat and listened to him talk - and fell totally in love.

JOE: Romantic.

ROBERT: Not really. Because after five minutes, Graham told me he was straight, "just to avoid any embarrassment or misunderstanding".

JOE: Oh! Did you believe him?

ROBERT: Did I bog roll. I was actually on a semi date that night. Awkward.

JOE: What did you do with "the semi"?

ROBERT: Oh. Brendan? No. Brandon. Or was it Brendan?

JOE: He must have felt truly valued.

ROBERT: I think he made his excuses and left?

JOE: I love it that happens, when you see that glow around two people, when they've just met and really hit it off, when suddenly no one else matters.

FX: Change of lights. Subdued. A Soho bar in 2000. The song is playing.

GRAHAM: It's been lovely meeting you. If I were gay, I'm certain you're just the kind of man I'd fancy /

ROBERT: That's an unusual thing to say.

GRAHAM: Is it?

ROBERT: For someone who's 100 per cent straight /

GRAHAM: Oh.

ROBERT: But being gay? Much as I fancy the pants off you, I wouldn't wish that on anyone.

GRAHAM: You seem to do fine. But I suppose gay life can be tough.

ROBERT: Just a bit. It is Graham, isn't it?

GRAHAM: Yes.

ROBERT: I'd love to see you again. Graham.

GRAHAM: Really? Yes. Likewise.

ROBERT: So?

GRAHAM: So, where might I find you?

ROBERT: I work most evenings in a bar on Wardour Street. The Pink Flamingo.

They shake hands. FX: Main lights back up.

JOE: The Pink Flamingo? Never heard of it.

ROBERT: No, I suppose not. "Standing in the door of the Pink Flamingo, crying in the rain". Lost on you. You really are starting to make me feel old.

JOE: And I'm not allowed to say sorry am I? So, he came to your bar?

ROBERT: Three nights later.

FX: Change of lights. Subdued. An alternative bar in 2000. Now to GRAHAM

Well, hello.

GRAHAM: Hi. Look, this is the first time I've ever been /

ROBERT: In such a hell hole?

GRAHAM: In a place of such sublime disrepute, packed to the nines with lubricious homosexuals.

ROBERT: Do you always talk like that?

JOE: Ha!

ROBERT: (*To Joe*) Ssssh.

GRAHAM: Well, yes, I suppose I do /

ROBERT: I think everyone in the room could see you were terrified, the moment you crossed our squalid threshold. (*Now to JOE*) The hours flew by. (*Now to GRAHAM*) So, again, good night.

GRAHAM: Yes. Thank you. I…

ROBERT: Yes?

GRAHAM: Um.

FX: Main lights back up.

JOE: Not even a hug?

ROBERT: Not even a hug.

JOE: Graham!

ROBERT: But I knew he'd be back.

JOE: Aha!

ROBERT: He was like a fragile, lost soul. So confident on the stage, playing someone else /

JOE: Never tried playing himself before?

ROBERT: Smart boy.

JOE: So you're the mysterious boyfriend!

ROBERT: I'm not that mysterious /

JOE: He's mentioned you. In passing.

ROBERT: How flattering.

JOE: He didn't say how handsome you are.

ROBERT: Stop it. Honestly. Somehow I knew he'd either make me the happiest man in the world, or break my heart into a million pieces.

JOE: Let me guess? Both?

ROBERT: You win the giant teddy bear. We were together for almost six months.

JOE: Love at first sight. I still don't know whether I really /

ROBERT: That's because you haven't experienced it yet. You will. Of course you will. Graham said it was the same for him. But it wasn't.

JOE: How do you know?

ROBERT: He doesn't like to make himself vulnerable. Not his style.

JOE: But how can you know?

ROBERT: He kept a diary. I saw him doing it. I knew it was wrong, but after we'd been together for a few weeks, my need to know could be denied no longer. I scratched the itch.

JOE: And?

ROBERT: And I looked at the diary entry for the first day we met:

GRAHAM: (*Or Robert*) "Chatted with one of the audience after the show. Robert. Must be careful."

JOE: You remember it word for word.

ROBERT: Of course I do.

JOE: "Must be careful"?

ROBERT: He was terrified of anyone knowing. Even himself.

JOE: (*Surprised*) Oh. Right. When was this again?

ROBERT: I was the gay Lorelei, luring him onto the rocks of debauchery.

JOE: Or pushing him to be him.

ROBERT: Maybe. His description, of course.

JOE: Huh?

ROBERT: The Lorelei, that /

JOE: Oh yeah, very Graham/

ROBERT: Very Graham.

JOE: Go on.

ROBERT: Well, the next night, we walked and talked for hours. Around 2am, I asked if I might kiss him.

JOE: You asked to kiss him. And he said?

ROBERT: He said yes.

JOE: Yay! Champagne moment!

ROBERT: Only because there was literally no one else around. Then I brought him back here and, after a night of unbridled passion, we emerged into the uncertain glory of an early autumn day – and the rest is *histoire*.

JOE: So this is your flat?

ROBERT: It was.

JOE: Sounds complicated.

ROBERT: Yes and no. In his diary over the next few days, Ham wrote about his difficult journey to rehearsals and the quirks of the other actors, then drinks in the Flamingo and there, buried in all the humdrum debris of a drab routine, one, short, life-changing sentence: "Today I tipped over and fell in love".

JOE: That's cute.

ROBERT: But it wasn't love at first sight. It was love at third shag.

JOE: Does it matter?

ROBERT: I think it does.

JOE: Perhaps you analyse too much.

ROBERT: Every night we had a kind of ritual. Three kisses. One for friendship – on the cheek – one for lust – on the lips – and one for eternal love. On the forehead.

JOE: That's cute.

ROBERT: You have a boyfriend?

JOE: Who says it would be a boy?

ROBERT: Oh, please.

JOE: Yeah, OK, it would be.

ROBERT: (*As Brucie*) Good gay, good gay!

JOE: Labels.

ROBERT: Suit yourself. Joe, love is the best thing in the world. Loving someone, being loved in return. Devoting your life to their fulfilment and happiness. Our salad days.

JOE: What happened?

ROBERT: He moved in with me. For a couple of months, it was absolute bliss. Then he started to... He wouldn't tell anyone. About us I mean. He wouldn't be honest.

JOE: But you were living together?

ROBERT: Officially he was just another "flat-mate". I begged him to be out and proud and sing it out loud, but No, No, Nanette.

JOE: Who?

ROBERT: The name of his favourite musical. Not because it's good. Because it's obscure. "Due a revival".

JOE: Why couldn't he be proud? Proud of you, proud of himself?

ROBERT: I think, because of his mother.

JOE: Isn't it always?

ROBERT: Eventually, he felt obliged to let her visit, with his sister. Pair of tub-thumping God botherers.

JOE: Sounds like a shit sit com. A "shit com".

ROBERT: We had to make out, one of us slept on the sofa bed. Every tiniest hint of coupledom, cosy domesticity – all swept under the carpet.

JOE: Fucksake.

ROBERT: At lunch, wine was taken. I still don't know why I did it.

JOE: What happened?

ROBERT: The wine spoke. If only I could go back. Make a different choice. *"Funny weather we're having. The Government, eh? Did you know I was named after Bobby Moore?"* If only I'd said all that. Instead of… instead of /

JOE: What did you say?

ROBERT: I told them what we were, Ham and I.

JOE: And?

ROBERT: Grim silence. They made their excuses and left.

JOE: Ouch.

GRAHAM: The sister had her toddler with her. On her way out, she prodded me in the chest and she said, "don't you ever come near my son again".

JOE: Charming. Surely they must have known?

ROBERT: Maybe, buried somewhere in the deepest, darkest corner of the family vault.

JOE: So Graham left too?

ROBERT: He did the washing up, then went to bed. It's ironic, really, because, that night, I really did sleep alone on the sofa bed. After that, he just kept pushing me away, always pushing me away.

JOE: But he did love you?

ROBERT: He loved me alright. He just didn't want to love me.

JOE: Oh, that's sad. And silly. Silly and sad.

ROBERT: That's when the letter arrived, from his sister, saying that he was dead to her. To make no further contact, unless and until he renounced me and "it".

JOE: I just don't get it.

ROBERT: I knew, if I left, he might have a chance of repairing things, of regaining his family. It broke his heart and it broke mine, but I had to hurt him.

JOE: Did he make it up with them?

ROBERT: No, but I had to give him that chance. After that I think he just gave up on the idea of happiness.

JOE: I think he's happier than he lets on? At least I hope he is.

ROBERT: I hope so too. And then he hit the gym big time.

JOE: Just what Soho needs – another Muscle Mary. Were you never tempted to call him?

ROBERT: Of course I was. But –

JOE: But?

ROBERT: Six months later I was at base camp. Joined the Army.

JOE: So what did Graham do?

ROBERT: Locked himself in the closet and swallowed the key.

JOE: But he was an ally, right? Went on Pride and stuff?

ROBERT: No way. He was petrified of anyone suspecting. And of contracting "the dreaded".

JOE: The dreaded.

ROBERT: The dreaded. Want to talk about it?

JOE: My mum kicked me out, when I was sixteen. Had to fend for myself for a bit. We're still estranged.

ROBERT: That's a Graham word.

JOE: A Graham word. I like Graham words. Mostly.

ROBERT: The man is like a walking thesaurus. And he doesn't half ram it down your throat. (*JOE pouts*). Oh, stop it.

JOE: My nan was the only one who kept in touch. She'd had a schoolfriend who was gay, when it was illegal and everything. She understood.

ROBERT: When you're young, you think everyone who's young, will always be young – and everyone who's old, has always been old.

JOE: We're talking again a bit. Now it's like the Christmas Day truce. Just without the carols, the footballs or the mud. Or truce, truth be told.

ROBERT: Mothers, eh? And now?

JOE: And now? Now I'm OK. I dreamed of being a playwright. Now I've sold my soul.

ROBERT: You appear not to have ditched the melodrama entirely.

JOE: I work for a US PR firm. Everyone there basically lives for cocaine and Moet –

ROBERT: You're still young. Time is on your side /

JOE: It's just how I am.

ROBERT: It's just how you are now.

JOE: I'm surrounded by total knobs and I think I've turned into one myself –

ROBERT: Then change. Do something worthwhile with your life.

JOE: Why thank you, Brené Brown.

ROBERT: Who?

JOE: Never mind.

ROBERT: Maybe you're right and you should feel shame about whatever the Hell it is you do. But imagine what it's like to feel shame, because of who you are, who you love – something you can't ever hope to change.

JOE: I know all about shame. And guilt.

ROBERT: Count your blessings, Joe. I need to go.

JOE: Stay. Stay for the party.

ROBERT: I can't.

JOE: You need to talk to Graham.

ROBERT: I can't.

JOE: It's your flat?

ROBERT: It was. Cherish your life, Joe. Live well. Be kind. It's never too soon to change and, in your case, it is certainly not too late.

JOE: Graham /

ROBERT: Graham will help. He always does, given the chance. And you, go fancy whoever you want.

JOE: Unless it's, like, a married man?

ROBERT: No, they're the best.

JOE: Please. Just for a bit.

ROBERT: I can't. Joe, so much unnecessary human misery is caused by a deficiency of love, a want of empathy and affection. We've all seen it. OK, society may judge you less now, but that doesn't make it easy – there's still the bullies, the preachers and the mothers, with their shattered dreams of perfect grandchildren, the fathers who think you're less of a man – or less than a man – the sympathy from friends who thank their lucky stars that it's not them. People will sense your vulnerability and exploit it mercilessly, try to persuade you that you are a "wrong 'un" – and that inevitably eats away at you, at your self-confidence and your self-esteem, in ways you don't even notice. But you'll be OK – you are OK. You'll just have to be a little bit tougher than most people will ever understand.

JOE: You'll come back?

ROBERT: I can never totally leave this place.

JOE: Please.

ROBERT: Just tell Ham, hello from Bobby.

Exit ROBERT. JOE heaves a deep sigh, bleakly contemplates the hedgehog, then sits down quietly for a moment.

SCENE 4 – CODA

GRAHAM enters. JOE springs up, looking guilty.

GRAHAM: Bugger me backwards, what a palaver!

JOE: Did you get your lah-de-dah wine?

GRAHAM: All they had, was the most expensive one. Sixty-nine quid. For one bottle. What's happened to the hedgehog?

JOE: I was distracted. You will not believe who just dropped by.

GRAHAM: Who? No, let me guess. West End Wendy Wilberforce. Since he moved to Camberwell I can't get rid of him.

JOE: It wasn't him.

GRAHAM: Jeremy then? No? Nicky? Spencer? Who?

JOE: Robert.

GRAHAM: Robert?

JOE: Robert! I met Robert!

GRAHAM: Robert? There's no Robert on the guest list.

JOE: Robert. Your Robert. (*He picks up a photo from the mantelpiece*) Him.

GRAHAM: Sorry, I don't understand.

JOE: Robert... was... here. Until, like, a minute ago. You just missed him. Lovely guy. I begged him to stay, but he wouldn't.

GRAHAM: Robert from that photo?

JOE: Yeah. Bobby.

GRAHAM: Bobby? Is this meant to be funny?

JOE: No. He said to tell you, "Bobby says hello".

GRAHAM: Ham?

JOE: Yeah, as in hammy acting. His joke.

GRAHAM: Are we done?

JOE: Look I know you haven't seen him for ages and everything, but I really think you should –

GRAHAM: What –

JOE: Get back together. Give it another shot.

GRAHAM starts clapping, sarcastically.

GRAHAM: Bravo, oh bravissimo. Please, take a bow. You bastards.

JOE: What?

GRAHAM: Who put you up to this?

JOE: No one put me up to anything.

GRAHAM: Oh really? So we're going to protract the façade? Streaming live, are we?

GRAHAM waves around the room.

JOE: No.

GRAHAM: Was it Keith? I bet it was.

JOE: Keith?

GRAHAM: It's just the kind of prank he'd come up with – oh yeah, clever – I'll give him that – but completely and utterly devoid of empathy.

JOE: Look, Bobby came in /

GRAHAM: Robert.

JOE: Alright, Robert came in, we sat down, we talked and he said, "Say hello to Ham". I really don't get what the problem is /

GRAHAM: You don't get what the problem is?

JOE: No, I don't. And why are we shouting?

GRAHAM: I'm shouting because he's dead.

JOE: Who's dead?

GRAHAM: Bobby is dead.

JOE: That is a problem.

GRAHAM: He joined the Army, took a bullet. End of.

JOE: I am so sorry.

GRAHAM: So was I.

JOE: I'm so confused right now. I think we just need to calm down /

GRAHAM: Leave. Now. You've had your fun.

JOE: No, no, no, no, no.

GRAHAM: Excuse me?

JOE: I am not leaving. Please, it's not a joke, I just want you to listen for one second. Please. Can we just take it down a bit? I swear on my life, he (*points at the photo*) was here. And we sat down and we had a good heart to heart. And he said to say hello. Look, there's a lot to process.

GRAHAM: (*In one breath, at speed*) A lot to process? You're telling me, the wandering spectre of the late love of my life, whom I've resented all these years for abandoning me, popped by, when I was out, for a friendly chat with someone I barely know? A lot to process? You think? You're leaving.

GRAHAM points to the door.

JOE: No, please don't do this. I need to understand what just happened. He, he told me all about the night you met – about the boring play /

GRAHAM: It was not boring /

JOE: I don't know, he said it was. And how you fell in love, and how you, how you singled him out, and he fell in love with you that night... and you worked at... the Pink Flamingo... and you

	met up there... and you, well you, you know... and you were confused and in the closet and then, then, you tipped over, you tipped over and fell in love with him. And you wrote that in your diary. Because Robert had a sneaky look. Couldn't help himself. Now tell me I'm imagining it all.
GRAHAM:	He really was here?
JOE:	He really was.
GRAHAM:	Is he alright?
JOE:	He looks alright. And he obviously adores you.
GRAHAM:	So why did he run off and put himself into danger, when he could have stayed safe, here with me?
JOE:	To protect you. He thought your family must come first.
GRAHAM:	My family? My family was him. He was all I cared about.
JOE:	After the big row. He thinks you pushed him away. Sorry. That's what he said –
GRAHAM:	When he left I couldn't forgive him, but part of me was relieved. Can you believe that? Relieved, because now I could hide again, go back to living the lie, a bit camp, no girlfriends, but not actually gay. I could hide again behind singledom, behind a pathetic pseudonym, behind all the front I'd put up. He thought he

could save me, but the truth is, I couldn't save myself. I was too afraid, too ashamed. I couldn't forgive him when he left. And I couldn't forgive him, when he died. And the truth is, there was nothing for me to forgive.

ROBERT enters. They cannot see him

What I should have said, is, "Bugger the world, and bugger my stupid, bigoted family. I'm proud of you, I love you so much, and I want the world to know about you and about us". But I didn't. I'm a coward. And I still miss him, so much.

GRAHAM crumples, sobbing. JOE hugs and consoles him.

JOE: You're not a coward. We all, you know, fight our own battles. These books, they're your weapons.

GRAHAM: They don't even have my real name on them.

JOE: Then we'll get them back into print, and this time with your real name on?

GRAHAM: Yeah. OK.

JOE: Right, you. Up you get.

ROBERT, without quite touching GRAHAM, lands a kiss onto his cheek, then onto his lips, then onto his forehead. GRAHAM is stunned, moved. Then ROBERT puts on the song. Then he exits. He might exit the room entirely, watch from some way off – or even sit amongst the audience. After a few moments, GRAHAM turns off the song.

SFX: The buzzer goes off

GRAHAM: I can't host a party, in this state.

JOE: Oh yes you can.

GRAHAM: Oh no I... Look at me. I'm a mess.

SFX: The buzzer goes off again

JOE answers the intercom, but says nothing.

A VOICE: Come on, Graham, get a move on, it's freezing out here.

GRAHAM: Oh. Barry. Always the first to arrive and the last to leave.

JOE: The hedgehog.

GRAHAM: Fuck the hedgehog.

JOE: Painful.

SFX: The buzzer goes off again, repeatedly.

GRAHAM: Alright, I'm coming, I'm coming.

A VOICE: Coming already? Good for you. Give that prehistoric prostate a practice, before it prolapses.

GRAHAM: Barry.

JOE: Barry. Right, you get the door and I'll get the music. It's party time.

As GRAHAM heads for the door, JOE squeezes his hand and their eyes meet for a moment. The lights fade and music continues to play, then stops abruptly.

THE END

I F____N' LOVE YOU

by Charlie Ross Mackenzie

A BEDROOM – LATE AT NIGHT

A sofa bed in a spare room. The bedclothes are ruffled and messed up but not pulled back. ADRIAN enters, wearing a dressing gown, and pyjama bottoms, he is drying his hair. Handsome, going a little grey. He sits down on his side of the bed. He picks up a pad and pen and starts taking notes. The Bucks Fizz song 'Land of Make Believe' is playing on a speaker on the bedside cabinet. He speaks to himself as he writes.

ADRIAN: Do you feel the Eurovision win has prevented you being taken seriously in the music business?

He strikes out what he has written down and starts again.

Is there a song you feel most proud of?

Simon enters. He is younger than Adrian. He is wearing pyjama bottoms and a trendy t-shirt. His hair is still wet and messed up. He jumps onto the bed.

SIMON: Alexa. (*Beat*) Shut the fuck up. You didn't hang about did you?

ADRIAN: This needs to get done.

As they chat, they make up the bed, fitting the sheet and putting on the duvet.

SIMON: How you getting on?

ADRIAN: Ok. It's just well, it's not as if they're the actual band is it?

SIMON: What, none of these guys are the actual Bucks Fizz?

ADRIAN: They've been mixed and matched so much over the years, now there's two of 'em.

SIMON: Two Bucks Fizzes?

ADRIAN: Now there's a collective noun I never thought I'd have to consider. Sort of. There's a mix of original and new members in each band, so makes them official-ish. They're like Trigger's broom.

SIMON: What?

ADRIAN: Trigger? Only Fools and Horses?

SIMON: Oh that, never watched it.

ADRIAN: I see, was it only the Sky at Night and the History of Monarchy at that fancy school?

SIMON: David Starkey? Are you kidding? Way too subversive. And anyway, we never watched much television. Too busy playing all that chess and rugger remember? What time's the interview?

ADRIAN: Either 10 or 2. They haven't confirmed yet.

SIMON has a quizzical look.

SIMON: Jeez, it's only a radio interview, shouldn't be this difficult. Need to be making their mind up.

ADRIAN giggles.

What?

ADRIAN: Your joke?

SIMON: What joke?

ADRIAN: Making your mind up?

SIMON: What are you talking about?

ADRIAN: Your youth is depressing.

SIMON rolls over beside ADRIAN. He gets close so that he can see what is on ADRIAN'S pad, leaning his head against his arm. ADRIAN barely moves, still focusing on the job. SIMON tosses and turns, struggling to get comfortable.

SIMON: Oh how much longer do we have to endure this?

ADRIAN continues working, half listening.

ADRIAN: Hmm?

SIMON: This fuckin' bed.

ADRIAN: Just one more night, posset. Unless you like the smell of paint stripper and freshly applied Dulux magnolia.

SIMON: It's a total pain.

ADRIAN: Oh suck it up, where's your resilience?

SIMON: We were never meant to be on this bed, this is just for guests.

ADRIAN: Revenge for dull dinner conversation. Now I know why they never come back.

SIMON: Exactly!

SIMON sits up suddenly.

SIMON: Did you hear that?

ADRIAN: What?

SIMON: That noise. It's that bloody mouse again.

ADRIAN throws the pad down onto the bed in despair.

ADRIAN: Oh for fuck's sake, how many times? We got it, it's dead. Gone. Bleedin' demised.

SIMON: No that was definitely a mouse noise.

ADRIAN: No it wasn't. I switched off the heating, it's the wood cooling down. Mice scratch and squeak, wood doesn't.

SIMON looks on edge, clearly scared of the possibility of a rodent.

SIMON: It could be.

ADRIAN: Well if it is a mouse maybe he's rewiring a plug or something.

SIMON: Don't be facetious.

ADRIAN: If we're lucky, maybe he'll tidy up your wardrobe.

SIMON picks up a pillow and smothers ADRIAN with it. They laugh and play fight for a bit then stop. SIMON cuddles into ADRIAN who picks up his pad again and gets back to work. ADRIAN tries to work for a bit but is clearly distracted by SIMON.

ADRIAN: Are you going to stay there?

SIMON: Huh?

ADRIAN: I'm trying to work.

SIMON: You never used to complain.

ADRIAN: I never complain when I'm not working. Haven't you got any work to do?

SIMON: Nah, I'll just do what I always do, wing it with cunning and guile. And of course, this.

SIMON points to his face and smiles.

ADRIAN: One day you'll get found out. Now get off.

SIMON reluctantly rolls away. He lies on his side of the bed and picks up his phone. He flicks through it. He looks over at ADRIAN, looks back at his phone and smiles.

SIMON: How do you know I'm not on Grindr right now?

ADRIAN: Because you have taste and a little class.

SIMON: YOU had Grindr when I met you!

ADRIAN: Yeah I know. (*Beat*) I'm scum, remember.

SIMON: Coming from a humble working class background does not make you scum.

ADRIAN laughs.

SIMON: What?

ADRIAN: I love that the middle classes look at the world like that. As if it's somehow noble to be poor and rise up from the mud like a Mick Lynch shaped phoenix.

SIMON: I didn't mean that. You aren't proud of what you've achieved?

ADRIAN: It was bloody hard work. Showbusiness is like a really tall ladder with two rungs on it, one at the top and one at the bottom. There's about six people at the top who get everything and the rest of us at the bottom praying for a crumb to fall down.

SIMON stares at ADRIAN

ADRIAN: Yes, I am proud. Thank you for reminding me that I should be.

They return their attention to previous activities. SIMON on his phone, ADRIAN working.

SIMON: I might get it. Just for fun.

ADRIAN: What?

SIMON: Grindr.

ADRIAN: Of all the things Grindr is, fun is not one of them. Like watching Downton Abbey when Maggie Smith's not in it.

SIMON: You should watch what you say. I could meet Hugh Jackman and run away with him.

ADRIAN: My god. I knew you were into older men, I just didn't think you were into old men.

SIMON: Ha. Ha. (*Beat*) It's not as if he's Ian McKellen.

ADRIAN: If it were McKellen I'd approve.

SIMON: He's an old man!

ADRIAN: He's statesmanlike.

SIMON: Can't argue with that.

ADRIAN: Ach!

ADRIAN, clearly frustrated, gets up.

> I swear I have a dysfunctional relationship, with my bladder.

SIMON: Well better that than with me. You do have the weakest bladder of anyone I know. I thought this was supposed to happen in, you know, really old age.

ADRIAN pauses, stares SIMON out and exits. SIMON picks up ADRIAN'S pad and reads over some of his notes. He reads them over. He shouts to ADRIAN who is offstage.

> This question about 80s music is good.

ADRIAN: (*OFFSTAGE*) What?

SIMON: I said the question about the 80s, I like it. People do go over the top about it. I bet it was nowhere near as cool as they say.

SIMON waits, there is no response.

> Are you alright in there?

A toilet flushes. ADRIAN enters.

> Look this is getting ridiculous, you have to get to a doctor and get that looked into.

ADRIAN: It's fine.

SIMON: It's not bloody fine. You need a pee more frequently than Boris Johnson has parties.

ADRIAN: You don't need to worry about me.

SIMON: I'm not, I'm worried about me. Every time you get up, I wake up. It's really pissing me off.

ADRIAN: Calm down. It's been like this forever. If it were something serious I'd be dead by now. It's like it has a mind and personality of its own. It wakes me up every night at 2:17. Then when I go, it makes me stand there for ages until IT wants to pee. Sometimes I have to shout at it.

SIMON: Is <u>that</u> what that is? You're shouting at your bladder?

ADRIAN: Well I aim the shout at my penis for obvious reasons, but it's my bladder I'm having a go at.

SIMON frowns.

> Oh don't give me the face. That fuckin' face.

SIMON: What face?

ADRIAN: That one. The disapproving face with the big cow eyes.

SIMON: I'm not doing a face, Ade.

SIMON'S frown and look of disapproval gets stronger.

ADRIAN: That's even worse. Jesus. Look, I know my body. When there's something to worry about, I'll do something about it.

SIMON: I'm just saying it might be worth an overhaul. You are over forty now. They may have to do *the* test.

ADRIAN: You can say it you know. Over forty? So that makes me forty eleven. And for the record, there's nobody going up there. I'll just die a painful and melodramatic death, thank you very much.

SIMON: What and leave me as the weeping widow?

ADRIAN: It's been like this my entire life. My bladder is an evil genius. It's like I'm Melania and my bladder is Trump. I'm stuck with an annoying selfish cunt forever. End of, now can we move on? I need to get this done. And no more of the Paddington hard stare please.

ADRIAN gets on with his work and SIMON picks up his phone again. He seems a little distracted.

SIMON: It was my regular face, Adrian, honest. I just worry, that's all. I've been here before.

ADRIAN: I know. Look I'll think about it. But I'm not having a stranger's finger up my arse, ok?

SIMON: I'm sure they'll say you're way too young to get that test anyway!

ADRIAN: I'm not going anywhere. So don't worry. Worrying is a waste of time and energy. It's like walking about /

SIMON: With an umbrella all the time expecting it to rain, yadda yadda. I know.

SIMON smiles. ADRIAN lays down on the bed and picks up his pad again.

ADRIAN: (*Cont'd*) Fucking Bucks Fizz.

SIMON: I've said it before, you shouldn't be doing this fluff. It's beneath you.

ADRIAN: Not according to Caroline it's not. Ever since Marsh-gate I've been stuck with this fluff.

SIMON: Marsh?

ADRIAN: Alex Marsh

SIMON: Oh yeah, Labour MP for Huddersfield.

ADRIAN: Lib Dems, Whitstable. But well done, you were close. I mean that was something over nothing. How can an MP be that sensitive?

SIMON: You called him a sanctimonious cunt?

ADRIAN: Not on air. And nobody disagreed with me. Anyway, since then it's been this banal shit all the way.

SIMON: You need to get back to the BBC.

ADRIAN: Not while you're there I won't.

SIMON: Different departments. And anyway I'm on telly.

ADRIAN: Oh, getting all high n' mighty are we?

SIMON: Pulling rank.

ADRIAN: Well you can just go and pull your /

SIMON: Can't you ever just sail by an innuendo?

ADRIAN: Nope. It's in my very soul. Brought up on a diet of Carry Ons and 'Are You Being Served?'.

SIMON: That's the one with the pussy jokes isn't it?

ADRIAN: Yes, well done.

SIMON: One day I'll be too old for you.

ADRIAN: Darling, that day passed when you turned 30. I only stay out of pity and the fact you couldn't afford the rent on this place alone. Even with your telly salary.

SIMON: Well I'm the one that wants to buy.

ADRIAN scowls.

SIMON: You <u>still</u> don't think we're 'there yet'?

ADRIAN: Well it's a big thing. It's not as if we don't already own property.

SIMON: Yes stuff we rent out, but it's not our property. I'm just saying we should look into it. Rent is a waste of money.

ADRIAN: What kind of mortgage would I get on a radio salary? We'd have to live in Tottenham!

SIMON: That's why you need to get back into television. I could put in a word.

ADRIAN: I'm not right for telly, and I don't even particularly like it. Isn't it just 'Love Island' development hell these days?

SIMON: It's not all like that.

ADRIAN: You're a presenter. And pretty. And like-able. I'm none of those things. And anyway, I couldn't bare to live in a world where 'The One Show' was a source of serious ambition. Plus, look at me. Not in the best shape for telly. I'm not exactly Chris Evans am I?

SIMON: Could be worse, you could be talking about ginger Chris Evans.

ADRIAN: I <u>was</u> talking about ginger Chris Evans.

SIMON gets up and exits.

SIMON: Need to brush my teeth.

SIMON exits. ADRIAN continues to work for a moment. From off stage SIMON'S voice can be heard.

Oh by the way, forgot to say, my agent got a call from 'Strictly Come Dancing'

ADRIAN jumps up.

ADRIAN: What? Shut... up!

ADRIAN goes over to the bathroom door.

What did you say?

SIMON replies with a toothbrush in his mouth.

SIMON: Nothing yet, just sounding me out. It's the early stages. They talk to at least thirty celebrities then whittle it down.

ADRIAN: God. And so you know, it's just 'Strictly'. *(ADRIAN does finger quotes)* The full title is passé. And not for nothing, they're playing fast and loose with the term celebrity these days.

SIMON: Oi.

ADRIAN: Come on, the dancers are more famous than the celebs.

SIMON: Cheeky.

ADRIAN: But seriously, you'd be great. You've got some moves.

SIMON: I dance like a rhinoceros on ice.

As SIMON enters again, ADRIAN grabs him in hold and starts to waltz, pulling him around the bed.

ADRIAN: See, it's like the King and I.

SIMON: The Queen and I more like.

They stumble and fall onto the bed.

ADRIAN: Still, good for the profile.

SIMON: Bloody hard work.

ADRIAN: When were you scared of hard work?

SIMON: You'd never see me.

ADRIAN: What? I'll be there in the audience, cheering you on. The camera cutting to me at key moments as I look simply fabulous.

SIMON: Ten years ago this would have been you.

ADRIAN: Are you saying I can't look fabulous anymore?

SIMON: No. Of course you can. But a few years back 'Strictly' might have been asking you.

ADRIAN: Yes, exactly and look what happened to me. The poof that time forgot.

SIMON: Oh I miss poof. Shame we're not allowed to say it anymore. It's a great word. Poof. Poof.

ADRIAN works and SIMON ponders.

SIMON: What's the plural of poof?

ADRIAN: Poofs I think.

SIMON: Isn't it like hoof, hooves. Pooves?

ADRIAN: Eh. No.

SIMON: There must be a collective noun surely? A brace of poofs? A palaver of poofs?

ADRIAN: A promenade of poofs? Seriously though, break legs to do this show.

SIMON: Hardly the correct phrase is it? Yeah I'll get Debs onto it. (*Beat*) Do you feel like you've failed? Because you haven't you know.

ADRIAN: Well not in an Alan Partridge way, no. But it's not where I expected to be. Regional radio with the occasional foray into Five Live and Radio 4 isn't exactly setting the heather alight is it? But it's work. That's the thing about this business. Everyone moans when they're out of work, then moan like Hell about the work when they get it.

SIMON: Countryfile.

ADRIAN: Huh?

SIMON: My ambition. It's not the One Show. It's Countryfile.

ADRIAN: No! You've never said.

SIMON: I think it would be, relaxing.

ADRIAN: That's how you see yourself? As the next John Craven? Actually when I say that out loud it sounds fine. The man is a legend.

SIMON'S phone pings. He picks it up and reads a text, puts it back and picks up his book. ADRIAN settles down, continues working. SIMON reads the text but after a moment gets distracted. He looks at ADRIAN who continues to work, SIMON tries to read again but becomes more and more agitated.

SIMON: Right, this isn't normal.

ADRIAN looks up bewildered.

ADRIAN: What have I done now?

SIMON: Nothing.

ADRIAN: Well that's outrageous, I'll pack my bags.

SIMON: It's not normal.

Beat

ADRIAN: Have you gone insane?

SIMON: No. We are a couple. It's not normal for me to get a text at this time of night and for you to neither care nor need to know what it was about.

ADRIAN: But... I don't. I honestly neither care nor want to know what it's about.

SIMON: Why the Hell not?

ADRIAN: Because if it was any of my business you would tell me.

SIMON: But it is your business.

ADRIAN: Ok, well, tell me then.

SIMON: You're supposed to ask. It's polite and caring.

ADRIAN: No. It's irritating and prying. But if it's going to help, then tell me.

SIMON folds his arms as if to go in a huff.

SIMON: No. It's fine.

ADRIAN: Are you really doing this?

SIMON: I just want you to take an interest.

ADRIAN: I do. But you need to have the right to keep things to yourself. As do I.

SIMON: Why, what are you hiding?

ADRIAN: Nothing. Oh my god, I was just thinking about Bucks Fizz, I didn't expect the Spanish inquisition.

SIMON: I'm just saying, who sits there saying nothing after his boyfriend has just got a text.

ADRIAN: A normal, balanced person?

SIMON: Tch.

SIMON turns and lies on his side with his back to ADRIAN. ADRIAN looks down at him. Takes a moment.

ADRIAN: Who was it then?

SIMON: Doesn't matter.

ADRIAN: Well, clearly it does.

SIMON: Just Michael.

ADRIAN: And? Is he ok?

SIMON sits back up.

SIMON: See that's it.

ADRIAN: Oh Christ.

SIMON: A normal, balanced person would wonder why anyone would text at this time.

ADRIAN: It's 10.45.

SIMON: Exactly.

ADRIAN: That's not late.

SIMON: Tch.

ADRIAN: So?

SIMON: What?

ADRIAN: Are you going to tell me what he wanted? Is he ok? As I see you're not leaping into your clothes and rushing to his assistance, I'm guessing it's nothing life threatening.

SIMON: It doesn't matter what it is. As is happens it is nothing, or rather he says he wants my advice on something. It's just the fact that you didn't care.

ADRIAN takes a breath.

ADRIAN: Ok, let me get this straight. You're annoyed because I didn't enquire as to the welfare of a friend who got in touch to ask you out for a cappuccino and a chat?

SIMON: Yes, but you didn't know that at the time did you? And I don't like cappuccino, why don't you know that?

ADRIAN: Have you actually gone insane?

SIMON: You drink Americano with cold milk, just a splash. Why don't you know what I drink?

ADRIAN: I do. I said cappuccino because it's a fun word to say, and makes my point better than a semi-hot hazelnut latte with an extra shot of chi and foam. Doesn't exactly trip off the tongue does it?

ADRIAN sits up and leans into SIMON. Props his chin on SIMON'S shoulder.

I'm ever so sorry.

SIMON smiles.

Now can I get back to Bucks Fizz?

SIMON: Yes. And I'm sorry too. I just worry about Michael. He lives in a land of make believe.

ADRIAN laughs.

SIMON: What?

ADRIAN: You did it again. With the song title.

SIMON: What song title?

ADRIAN: Are you taking the piss?

ADRIAN returns to work. SIMON picks up a book from the bedside cabinet. It's 'Catcher in the Rye'. He reads for a page.

SIMON: You know what?

ADRIAN doesn't look up from his work.

ADRIAN: What?

SIMON: I'm starting to think this book is utter shit. Everyone bangs on about it as if it's a big deal but it's just whiny self-indulgent twattery.

ADRIAN: Insightful review.

SIMON: It's like Citizen Kane.

ADRIAN stops again, takes off his glasses and sits up with a slight sigh.

SIMON: Everybody says it's their favourite movie when it's actually Deadpool. Everyone who owns 'A Brief History of Time' has only read one chapter. When I tried I may as well have read it backwards for all I understood. That's the problem these days. Everyone is desperately trying to be something they're not. Multiple personalities all over the place. There's your online personality, the one for friends and family, and your real one. And almost nobody gets to know that one. That's why the little things are so important. It's the small things that make us… real. Why can't we all just be honest? Deadpool IS better than Citizen Kane and I'd rather be reading Harry Potter and the Goblet of Fire again than this pretentious shit.

SIMON stops and realises ADRIAN is staring at him.

What?

ADRIAN: You done?

SIMON: I think I'll start something else. Any recommendations?

ADRIAN: Try reading some Philip K. Dick?

SIMON: Oh I'm always up for a bit of...

ADRIAN: Aww, a Carry On line... I'm so proud.

SIMON: I was going to say science fiction. I've read quite a lot of sci-fi. Brave New World, 2001, the Bible.

SIMON'S phone pings again. They both stop and look at each other. SIMON slowly reaches for his phone. ADRIAN throws down his pad and sits up.

ADRIAN: Wait! Stop, wait just one damn moment, I must bait my breath.

SIMON: Piss off.

SIMON picks up his phone and looks at the text.

Oh fuck.

ADRIAN: What? You mean this one actually is something?

SIMON: He thinks Joe is having an affair.

ADRIAN: Yeah I imagine he probably is.

SIMON: How can you say that?

ADRIAN: Come on, that pair give frivolity a bad name. They're both one Bacardi Breezer away from being on Judge Rinder.

SIMON picks up the phone and replies. ADRIAN gets up.

SIMON: Not the bladder again?

ADRIAN: No. I'm a bit hungry.

SIMON smiles with a twinkle in his eye.

SIMON: All that exercise got you famished?

ADRIAN: I'm going to get a biscuit. Want one?

SIMON shakes his head.

SIMON: You've never liked Joe have you?

ADRIAN: (VO) I don't not like him. It's you who doesn't like him.

SIMON: That's not true.

ADRIAN enters eating a custard cream.

ADRIAN: Oh come on, you don't exactly hold back do you? Last time we met them you engineered a discussion on Welsh independence, just to wind him up.

SIMON: Oh, did I?

ADRIAN: You know damn well you did. And anyway, you'll never be happy until Michael goes out with someone called George.

SIMON: Well come on, how cool would that be?

SIMON finishes the text.

ADRIAN: He came on to me once you know?

SIMON: George Michael?

ADRIAN: No. Michael, your Michael. About four weeks after we met. Bold as brass, and in your own living room as well.

SIMON: Oh?

ADRIAN: Yeah, you'd nipped back out to get some wine. He sat down beside me, got all up close and personal. I tried moving away but he insisted. Then apropos of nothing, the hand slipped onto my leg. Ran the tips of his fingers ever so slowly up my thigh, looked me in the eye, and, cheesy as you like, said, 'Well then?' You believe that? 'Well then?' Not exactly James Bond is it? And he thinks he's a right old Casanova as well.

SIMON: And then what happened?

ADRIAN: I did what every self-respecting gay man should do when his new boyfriend's mate comes onto him. Had a quick shag and opened another bottle of wine.

SIMON: Wha /

ADRIAN: Ha! Course I didn't. Told him to piss off, the cheeky little fucker.

SIMON: Quite right.

ADRIAN gets onto the bed again. He stops for a moment, looks at SIMON, takes a thought.

What?

ADRIAN: You don't seem that... bothered.

SIMON: Well it's just Michael isn't it? He needs to know that everyone fancies him.

ADRIAN: I don't.

SIMON: Clearly. It's just not that surprising.

ADRIAN: Strange few months those. I'd never had that much attention. Like, ever. In my clubbing days, and believe me they didn't last long, I was always the one waiting until 3am to catch the last drunken, desperate train out of the station. Then wham, within four weeks, you, then Michael.

SIMON: Why is that so shocking?

ADRIAN: Because, well, I mean I'm, me, and you're, ya know... you. It was just strange.

SIMON: What do you mean 'I'm me'? Why do you always bring it down to looks? And by the way, you are good looking but there is a little more to it. Or is that it? Is that why you're with me?

ADRIAN: What? No, be quiet.

SIMON: No, seriously. What if my looks go? What if I get a little flabby? People like me are notorious for not hanging on to their looks. Look at Brendan Fraser.

ADRIAN: Who?

SIMON: Exactly. So? What if I lose it all. Get old.

ADRIAN: What if you get old? Sorry to break this to you my dear but there's no stopping that train.

SIMON: You know what I mean.

ADRIAN: We still shag. We still kiss. We still spoon. Most importantly, we still laugh. I can honestly live without any of the others, but the last one. That's the clincher. And from what I hear there is nothing more hilarious than an old man trying to have sex, so I think we're Ok.

SIMON: For now.

ADRIAN: So, as long as we keep laughing.

SIMON laughs, lies down with his eyes open staring upwards. ADRIAN continues working.

You got much to do?

ADRIAN: You want to go to sleep?

SIMON: No, it's fine. I'll drift off in time.

SIMON kisses ADRIAN softly and sweetly.

ADRIAN: (*Cont'd*) I'm done in anyway. Bucks Fizz can just get a taste of the Simon Collins style of winging it.

SIMON: Cunning and guile?

ADRIAN: Yeah. Plus I need some sleep. They want photos for the website and if I don't get a proper kip I'll look like the back end of a bus.

SIMON: Yip, the camera never lies.

ADRIAN: Oh come the fuck on!

SIMON: Seriously, what?

ADRIAN: Good night.

They both put out their respective bed lights.

SIMON: Do you think we'll ever be that couple who just go to bed, kiss goodnight, sleep and never have sex?

ADRIAN: I kind of think that's inevitable don't you?

SIMON: Really? Such a cliche isn't it? I mean, that whole, oh we have so much more than sex. Companionship is everything. You not think it's a bit of a cop out?

ADRIAN: How do you mean?

SIMON: That acceptance that all relationships are doomed to become a sexless friendship, bogged down in debt and a mortgage. It's easier to stay than to just acknowledge that maybe it's over and move on.

ADRIAN: Are you trying to say something?

SIMON: What? Oh no, shit no, I mean, I hope we keep doing it forever. But, I mean, if it goes, the passion, the fancying each other, isn't it better to just say that?

ADRIAN: Where's this come from?

SIMON: Dunno. Just a thought. I'm a realist.

ADRIAN: Well frankly I'd rather you were less pragmatic at this time of night.

SIMON: Every relationship I know has ended up like that. My parents, some mates, even my sister says she and Phil never do it anymore.

ADRIAN: You talk about stuff like that with your sister?

SIMON: Yeah. Don't you?

ADRIAN: Oh no my family never talked about feelings or emotions. We were quite presbyterian when it comes to stuff like that. Even hugs were out of bounds.

SIMON: That's so tragic.

ADRIAN: Isn't it? My parents had separate rooms for as long as I can remember. And that's all I ever knew. Even on telly. 'Terry and June' always had single beds, so did Basil and Sybil. It's odd, there was always this talk about promoting homosexuality but when I was growing up it felt like the only people I ever saw in a double bed together were two men. Eric and Ernie. Laurel and Hardy. Heterosexual life looked so stagnant.

ADRIAN glances over at SIMON who has drifted off to sleep. He smiles, leans in, strokes his hair gently. He turns over.

An hour later.

ADRIAN gets up. He whispers to himself.

ADRIAN: (*Cont'd*) Fuck. Off.

He gets up and makes his way to the bathroom. He creeps back in trying to stay quiet but stubs his toe.

>Jesus, shit Christ

SIMON jumps up, ripped from his sleep. Flustered, he puts on his light.

SIMON: What is it?

ADRIAN: My toe. Every bloody night. This stupid bed.

SIMON: Yeah you're right, it's the bed that's stupid.

ADRIAN: How can something so seemingly innocuous be so bloody painful?

SIMON: You mean like Westlife?

ADRIAN cuts SIMON a look as he hobbles back to bed.

>They were like that, Westlife. Just, blah. You know, like an old person in front of you in the post office queue. You don't hate them, you just wish they weren't fuckin' there.

ADRIAN: No you go on having a nice little chat with yourself.

SIMON: What?

ADRIAN: I'm fine by the way.

SIMON: You think it's broken?

ADRIAN: Well I'm not sure. Not since the extensive diagnosis and x-ray I got in the last 80 seconds.

SIMON: No need to be like that.

ADRIAN: Go back to sleep.

SIMON: I wasn't asleep. Not really. Couldn't.

ADRIAN massages his foot while SIMON lies back.

Insomnia is a curse. Way worse than a stubbed toe. Maybe hell is like insomnia. Just endlessly tossing and turning, forced to think of all the errors we've made in life, forever, for eternity.

ADRIAN: Well what with your philosophising and my broken bones, nobody is getting any sleep here tonight. Ooh, this is shit.

SIMON sits up purposefully.

SIMON: I asked him to do it.

ADRIAN: Asked whom to do what?

SIMON: Come on to you. Michael. It was me, I asked him to.

ADRIAN: Wha... how.

SIMON: I don't know why really. It sounded like a good idea in my head. It's just that I really liked you and I wanted to be sure.

ADRIAN: Sure of what?

SIMON: I was a well known face on TV, so I wanted to, you know, make sure you were the real thing and not just a celebrity fucker. So I thought maybe I'd, I dunno, test you.

ADRIAN: You thought you'd test me?

SIMON: Look it's not that bad when you think about it. Michael told me you were appalled – in fact he was totally pissed off by that - and then I knew.

ADRIAN takes a moment.

ADRIAN: You tested me??

SIMON: It's been really bugging me and I wanted to get it out there. And since you mentioned it I…/

ADRIAN: I can't believe this.

SIMON: Well you never said either.

ADRIAN: I didn't want to come between you and your mate, plus I had no idea at the time what kind of relationship you two had. But, a test. Of all the sly, distrustful little tricks.

SIMON: Oh shit, you're angry. I get that. But when you think about it, it's kind of funny. See, ha. It's funny. Kind of.

SIMON puts on his winning smile.

ADRIAN: Oh no, don't think that's going to get you out of this.

ADRIAN stands up quickly.

ADRIAN: Kind of funny… Oww.

He remembers his injury, but this doesn't stop him trying to get to SIMON. ADRIAN crawl across the bed and SIMON runs round it.

Don't you run away from me ya little shit.

SIMON: Careful you might hurt your foot.

ADRIAN: It'll be absolutely fine when my foot is pressing down on your neck.

SIMON: Now come on, calm down. Don't get all, Scottish on me.

ADRIAN: Away an' fuck yourself.

SIMON: That's what I meant.

There is a ridiculous and farcical altercation between them which ends with them both under the duvet and entangled in them.

If you would just let me explain.

ADRIAN: Explain what? Have you been doing this for years? Everyone and anyone who's ever chatted me up has been a Simon set up?

SIMON: Of course not. (*Beat*) Why, who else has been chatting you up?

ADRIAN: That's it. You're going to get it.

SIMON: Violence is not the answer.

ADRIAN: Cunning and fuckin' guile right enough.

SIMON: Unduvet me man!

ADRIAN releases the duvet and SIMON stands up. ADRIAN remains entangled on the bed, he uses the duvet as a barrier to demonstrate his huff.

Before I met you, my love life was one disaster after another.

ADRIAN: Oh come on!

SIMON: You see that's it, everyone thinks that because I'm, eh /

ADRIAN: Drop dead gorgeous? Boo fuckin' hoo.

SIMON: Eh, yeah, em, that. Well, yes everybody thinks that it's all dead easy. You want to know the amount of nights I would go out alone for a drink and nobody would speak to me? I would see them all, drifting about, obviously wanting to talk to me and /

ADRIAN: And thinking you were out of their league? Yeah, been there. Drifting out in mediocre land with the rest of the mere mortals.

SIMON: Maybe we could live without the self-deprecation. It's me who's talking. For once.

ADRIAN sits quietly and zips his mouth shut.

SIMON: I mean, I'm not looking for sympathy. I'm well aware that I've had it easier than most. Never wanted for anything, Jesus, even coming out was straightforward. My parents got exactly what they wanted: three children, one of each. School was relatively straight forward. Sex was never an issue. But meeting someone? Boy. I'm useless at chatting up, I just don't have the lines. So yes, I would see you all out there, desperate for someone to step up and just say hello. Most nights I'd go home alone. This is going to sound ridiculous, but looks can be a curse you know.

ADRIAN cuts him a look of incredulity.

SIMON: I mean it. One look and up pops the fake smile. Or the assumption of happiness.

ADRIAN: While the rest of us have to fall on the 'looks are only skin deep' sword.

SIMON: 'It's the personality that matters'.

ADRIAN: Nobody ever had a wank over a personality.

SIMON: Quite. Then when I got 'Blue Peter', I had a procession of guys all wanting to be with the TV lad. Every one of them turned out to be a loser. Not one interested in me, who I am. Until you.

ADRIAN: What?

SIMON: Yes, you. You didn't give a shit. The first time I met you, remember, that stupid cocktail party? The one where Shane Richie tried to do a handstand against Anthea Turner and broke her nose?

ADRIAN lets a giggle out but then suppresses it.

SIMON: Finally, I met someone who talked. To me. You asked me about me. Not what I did, not what it was like being on the telly, or who's banging whom. You wanted to know about me.

ADRIAN: Well, that's because you seemed interesting.

SIMON: Exactly. Not a quick fuck or a conquest.

ADRIAN: Yeah but you thought that was me chatting you up. I had no idea that's what I was doing. I mean why would I think I had any chance… you know?

SIMON: And that's exactly why I asked you out. After a few weeks I just got wondering if it was all just flannel, you know, a routine.

ADRIAN: I'm really not that organised.

SIMON: No, you're not. And I know that now. But not then.

ADRIAN: Who has that kind of patience? Not me.

SIMON: Exactly. And yes, I did let Michael get inside my head. It was even his stupid bloody idea. In fact that's where it backfired on him. He couldn't believe you knocked him back.

ADRIAN grudgingly smiles.

Look, it was stupid and immature. But it was three years ago. You know what I was like then.

ADRIAN: A bit of a /

SIMON: / A twat.

ADRIAN: Wouldn't go that far.

SIMON: But it did reassure me that my instincts were right. That I could trust you.

ADRIAN: Well, you're just lucky you weren't friends with Zac Efron.

SIMON: If I were friends with Zac Efron I wouldn't /

ADRIAN: Don't push your luck, mate!

SIMON sits on the bed beside ADRIAN.

SIMON: Why is this shit so complicated?

ADRIAN: Because we don't live in a Richard Curtis movie.

SIMON: Thank god for that.

ADRIAN: Doesn't seem so complicated for others, though. I'd see everyone else with boyfriends, girlfriends, getting married and I'd just think, how? I mean how are you all doing this? Was there a training day in school and I missed it? Did I sleep in or something? Or maybe I was in the toilet. My bladder again.

SIMON: I never had a problem getting boyfriends, girlfriends.

ADRIAN looks at SIMON.

Don't give me that look, you know there were girls.

ADRIAN looks a little sheepish.

Sorry, I didn't mean to, well, my point is, getting someone to go out with you doesn't necessarily mean that you're any good at it. I was awful. I'd miss birthdays, forget dates.

ADRIAN: So what's happened here then?

SIMON: Maybe our equal ineptitudes cancel each other out? Or maybe we just really and truly lo /

ADRIAN: Woah, just wait a moment there mister. You know the rules.

SIMON: Really?

ADRIAN: Yes, really.

SIMON: When are you going to get the fuck over this?

ADRIAN: Over what? I think it's fairly reasonable.

SIMON: What? Not being allowed to tell the most important person in my life how I feel?

ADRIAN: Yes. It changes everything. Usually for the worse.

SIMON: In what possible way could saying that one little word change things so badly?

ADRIAN: Because it's not one little word is it? It's one enormous fuck up of a four letter word. It's just chucked out there. As if saying it will cover everything else up. My dad used to say it all the time to my mum and it meant nothing. Empty words. Actions. Deeds. That's what we've got.

SIMON: But telling someone how you feel is a basic, no, a primal, way of expressing yourself. And it's always good to hear.

ADRIAN: Every time in my life when someone had said that to me, and that's not many, it turned out to be a lie. A pre-amble to disaster.

SIMON: You think I'd be lying?

ADRIAN: No. But it's, a state of mind. Of being. I feel it from the second I come home at night. Don't you? Every time you text me. Every time you say something daft, or want to watch "Love Island". I feel it. Every time you tell me off, every time you make me a cup of tea, every time I look at you. I feel it. And for me, that's enough. When it's said. When it's out there. There is always a chance that it isn't meant. But if you feel it all the time the way I do, well, does it need to be said anyway?

SIMON gently strokes ADRIAN'S hair.

And then what happens? It's said, and then it keeps on being said. Until one week it's said less. Then a week becomes a month and so on and so on, and before you know it, only on birthdays and Christmas cards. It's not saying the word I object to. It's the possibility that one day you'll stop saying it.

SIMON: You, old man, are off your head.

ADRIAN: Oh I know, totally bonkers. I'm sorry, and I know how you feel about this, but, like we said, this isn't a Hollywood movie. For the first time in my life, I'm in a relationship and totally confident about it. Every other relationship I've been in has been straight to DVD, but this time, all the crazy? It doesn't seem to matter. Not to you. That's how I know.

SIMON: How's your toe?

ADRIAN: Bloody sore. But it's fine. Because you're here.

They smile.

SIMON: I'm sorry about Michael.

ADRIAN: Do you mean for coming onto me, or just in general?

SIMON: Both.

ADRIAN: Haven't you heard back from him? No more drama?

SIMON: No, actually. I hope he's ok. He might be a pratt but he's the pratt I've known the longest.

ADRIAN: Well, for what it's worth I do too. I mean they are kind of right for each other. And so long as they're together it keeps both of them both out of circulation and everyone else is spared.

SIMON gets up, picks up his phone from the bedside cabinet and checks it. ADRIAN continues rubbing his foot.

SIMON: Nope, nothing. You want a pill for that?

ADRIAN: Got any ecstasy?

SIMON: Oh how 90s.

ADRIAN: Don't knock the 90s. Apart from the Lighthouse Family it was pretty good.

SIMON: All went tits up though didn't it? Britpop, New Labour, even the President was allowed to get blow jobs in the Oval office. It was all going so well. Then Diana died and it all went wonky.

ADRIAN: Then David Bowie died and EVERYTHING went wrong. Could it be that David Bowie really was holding the fabric of the universe together?

SIMON: What is it with you and that man?

They both switch off lights, give each other a small kiss and settle down. They lie spooning into each other.

FADE TO BLACK. THEN FADE UP.

Time has passed, SIMON lies on his side, ADRIAN is on his back facing up, his eyes are open. ADRIAN sits up suddenly. He prods SIMON gently.

ADRIAN: Si. Si. You asleep?

SIMON: Yes.

ADRIAN: No, really.

SIMON: Yes, really, I really am asleep.

ADRIAN: I've been thinking.

SIMON: Never a good idea.

ADRIAN: No seriously, this is important.

SIMON: I'm sure it can wait.

ADRIAN: No, it can't. I need to ask you something.

This gets SIMON'S attention. He sits up, half asleep and dishevelled. He looks at ADRIAN.

SIMON: Well?

ADRIAN: We should get a dog.

SIMON looks around the room.

ADRIAN: What are you doing?

SIMON: Looking for a heavy object to hit you with.

ADRIAN: No honestly, it's exactly what we need.

SIMON: You are completely ridiculous.

ADRIAN: What? You like dogs.

SIMON: Hmmm. It's four in the fucking morning. These are conversations that can wait.

SIMON turns over again, trying to get some sleep. ADRIAN remains sat up. A moment passes.

ADRIAN: When I was a kid we always had a dog.

SIMON: Here we go.

ADRIAN: Good for the soul. No idea why we had one. Mum could barely feed the kids, but we had Barney. I named him. After Barney Rubble. From 'The Flintstones'. Daft little mutt. I think she knew we needed him because he brought smiles into the house. Weren't that big on smiling. My family. Truth be told we weren't that big on family. Just four people living in the same house with not much in common. Apart from being skint of course. Dad liked a drink /

SIMON: A lot of drink /

ADRIAN: Mum tried to keep it all together and my brother was an arsehole.

SIMON: A real arsehole /

ADRIAN: Everyone walked on eggshells around him, not knowing which way his mood would swing from one minute to the next. He would taunt me. All the time, relentlessly. And I would just take it. Because it was the easy thing to do. Like my mum did. She always took his side.

SIMON: It's bizarre the paths some people choose to take just because it's the smoother road. Even if it hurts others.

ADRIAN: Yeah, it was the easy thing to do. Oh he could be ok some of the time. He was a huge Queen fan and I adored Bowie.

SIMON: No. Really? Odd how that has never come up.

ADRIAN: Tch. Well we would argue all the time about who was the best. Bowie's had more number ones I would say. Queen play to bigger crowds he would say. On and on and on. Then one day we read that it was happening. Queen and David Bowie were to collaborate. I thought for a moment that it would bring us together, make us closer, you know? Like brothers should be. Then 'Under Pressure' came out and it was amazing. Uplifting, spiritual even. Truly worthy of their genius. Yeah, I liked Queen too but would never admit that to Callum. So when 'Under Pressure' went to number one, well that was it. Affirmation that we were both right. Our guys were both at the top of the tree. Maybe we would be proper brothers now. Perhaps get on just that little bit better. But what did we do? Argued over whose bits of the song were the best. And the bullying and the moods and the getting his own way just continued. That was the moment I checked out of the whole family thing. I left, went to university, came out… and we just never really talked again. The occasional wedding, funeral, birthday party. Then, at thirty-six, he had the car crash. So, in the end, after all that arguing and bickering, I got my own way. I won.

SIMON has slowly sat up and listened to ADRIAN. He leans over and hugs ADRIAN.

SIMON: What a tale to tell. (*Beat*) But then I have heard it five times already.

ADRIAN: I still can't believe is that everyone was shocked when Freddie Mercury came out. 'He's so gay' I would say to my brother. 'No he's fuckin' not,' he protested. It's odd the way people simply refuse to believe what is right in front of their eyes.

SIMON: Social programming isn't it? They project who they are onto everyone else and make automatic assumptions.

ADRIAN: Yeah I know. Do you remember last Christmas Eve when I went out to do some last minute shopping. Three times the shop assistants said to me, 'oh did you forget about the missus'? It never occurs to them that I might not be your standard married man with two point four kids. So what do you do? Just nod and smile. And let them think that they live in this nice little safe world where everyone is just like them. Take the easy road.

SIMON gets up.

SIMON: Now, I want a biscuit.

SIMON exits.

ADRIAN: Dogs bring smiles.

SIMON enters, eating a biscuit.

ADRIAN: So?

SIMON: What?

ADRIAN: Will we get a dog?

SIMON: Are we really doing this now?

ADRIAN: Why not?

SIMON: Yes.

ADRIAN: You're just saying that so that you can get back to sleep.

SIMON: Oh well worked out Miss Marple. You can see right through me.

ADRIAN: It's alright for you, bet you had loads of dogs in that ridiculous house you grew up in.

SIMON: We only had two.

ADRIAN: Oh just the two. And didn't they make you smile?

SIMON: Well if you must know.

ADRIAN: What?

SIMON: I wasn't really that bothered.

ADRIAN: NO.

SIMON: This may come as crushing blow to you but not everyone likes hairy beasts who jump everywhere and dribble all over you.

ADRIAN: You don't complain when I do that.

SIMON: You're not that hairy and your jumping days are very much behind you.

ADRIAN: I suppose with all that room you barely noticed them. Who walked them, Jeeves?

SIMON: You really do think I grew up in an E.M. Forster novel don't you?

ADRIAN: Oh come on, you did a bit. Your parents have a gravel driveway. That's the very definition of posh.

SIMON: Well since you mention it, I was away at that posh school remember? So I didn't get a chance to bond with Coco and Claret.

ADRIAN: Coco and Claret.

ADRIAN laughs, remembering the names.

SIMON: They were Mummy's... My Mother's dogs really.

ADRIAN: Oh good old Damaris. She is a good laugh your Mum. Once she got past the disapproval.

SIMON: There never was any disapproval. That my neurotic one, is all in your mind. Plus she is insufferable when she's on one of her projects. And I know what she's like, why use three or four words when a couple of thousand would do?

ADRIAN: Hey, be nice. I wish I had a living Mum who was insufferable you know.

SIMON: No. Not allowed. You've used up your dead mother quota for this month.

ADRIAN: I thought that was number three?

SIMON: Five.

ADRIAN: Shit.

SIMON: So anyway, my parents are way more liberal than you think.

ADRIAN: Your dad said he wanted to hunt Jeremy Corbyn through the streets with a Mauser rifle!

SIMON: That was after a few too many sherries. He's a big pussycat really. Thinks you're great.

ADRIAN: So you say. He doesn't quite trust me though, thinks I'm in on the socialist revolution.

SIMON: At some point, you're really going to have to get over this working-class bullshit you know. You are such an inverted snob.

ADRIAN: I am not.

SIMON: Come on, you make Christopher Eccleston look like Prince Philip.

ADRIAN: It's social conditioning.

SIMON: It's social bullshit. I know that my journey here was a bit easier than yours. I was born in the room. But that doesn't mean the good guys and the bad guys are easy to spot. It's not that delineated. And what's more, you know that too. Look at where you are, where you've got to. You did this. You said it yourself, when you were growing up everyone else got their own way. But you played the long game. You won.

ADRIAN puts his head in SIMON'S lap. SIMON strokes his hair.

ADRIAN: It's about leaving a mark isn't it?

SIMON: What?

ADRIAN: Life. All of it. I mean isn't that all we want. As the years go by I can't stop wondering how I'll be remembered. What mark will I leave?

SIMON: Like having children I suppose.

ADRIAN sits up. He looks into SIMON'S eyes, strokes his hair back and kisses his forehead with great affection.

ADRIAN: My career has been my family. For the most part. I got into broadcasting so that I could speak. To say something. Do something. Try to make a difference. I wanted to be brave. To be bold. You know what I did? I took the easy path. Just like my bloody mother. And god knows how many people got hurt because I didn't have the balls to say the right thing. It's easy to say I won because I have good job, a nice house. (*Beat*) You.

They both smile.

ADRIAN: But when all is said and done, the victory seems hollow. I could have – and should have done so much more.

SIMON: That would all be very touching if it wasn't such a load of nonsense.

ADRIAN: Wha /

SIMON: Brian Fletcher. A 72 year old pensioner who was being so screwed by energy companies, got no help from the department of work and pensions, scared to heat his house and nearly died from the cold. You were told about it by his neighbour and you reported on it. You got him the help and support he needed.

ADRIAN: How did you /

SIMON: / Angela Gardiner. Had an affair with a cabinet minister and when it ended was run out of Westminster, lost her job and had her name dragged through the mud. Your report revealing a series of other affairs helped to give her some kind of life back.

ADRIAN looks at SIMON

ADRIAN: Wow, you remembered all of that?

SIMON: Of course I bloody remember. What kind of man do you think I am? I don't just swan in and out of your life and cherry pick the bits that suit me. This is an investment you know.

ADRIAN: I'm sorry I /

SIMON: / I do occasionally read your Wikipedia page. I'm amazed you don't. You have made a difference. You think it stops there? Have you any idea how many other Brians and Angelas see stories like the ones you chased and then act themselves. We do want to leave our mark. We just don't always have the luxury of bearing witness to it.

ADRIAN contemplates for a moment.

    Clarence.

ADRIAN: Cross-eyed lion.

SIMON: No. The dog, I think he should be called Clarence.

ADRIAN sits up, smiles and kisses SIMON.

ADRIAN: What if it's a she?

SIMON: Magenta.

ADRIAN laughs.

SIMON: I better not get stuck walking the little shit all the time.

ADRIAN: Who said little? I want a huge one. I'm not gonna be one of those muscle Marys out on Hampstead Heath walking a permed rat.

SIMON: This could end our sex life you know.

ADRIAN: Well we've had a good run.

SIMON: Speak for yourself.

ADRIAN: It'll be fine. Career, dog, no sex life. It's like being straight. All we need now are the kids.

SIMON slumps a little.

I'm sorry, I didn't mean /

SIMON: / no it's fine.

There is an awkward moment.

You shouldn't have to /

ADRIAN: / I know but still.

ADRIAN takes SIMON'S hand.

You know that you've never actually told me what happened.

SIMON: Yes I have.

ADRIAN: No.

SIMON: I have.

ADRIAN: No. You really haven't. Your mum told me some. You've never really told me anything. I mean it's ok, and now's definitely not the /

SIMON: / We were pretty stupid. The way you are when you're young. And the girlfriend thing was never going to last. Eight months after we'd split, there she was. Little bundle of /

SIMON holds back his emotion.

ADRIAN: You don't have to /

SIMON: No, it's fine. Those next three years were all over the place. At the end I was in Manchester and they were in Cardiff. I'd been travelling back and fore to the hospital. I was a mess. At work I could barely focus on anything. But there I was, smiling away for the camera. Doing my bit. Funny, the show you can put on when you have to. Then one day I got a call from Sophie. She said I better get there as soon as possible. (*Beat*) Do you really need to hear this now?

ADRIAN: No. But I do think you need to say it.

SIMON: I started to get my stuff together and realised that I would be away for a while. Work told me to take as much time as I needed. Then I had this thought, this desperate, tragic thought. Should I take a suit? A tie? You have no idea what it's like to prepare for a funeral of someone who isn't dead yet. I went through all the scenarios. I'll just come back and get it. I'll buy a new one. In the end, the head rules the heart. We English, we're so fucking... practical. So I duly folded it into my case. In the end, it was one less thing to think about at a time when you don't want to think about anything.

SIMON looks at ADRIAN and strokes his cheek.

I'm sorry I haven't told you. I should have. And I will. But maybe that's all for now eh?

ADRIAN: Yeah. Enough. Enough.

ADRIAN leans in and kisses SIMON sweetly.

SIMON: You know who loves dogs?

ADRIAN: Who?

SIMON: Children.

ADRIAN: Say what?

SIMON: Why don't we then?

ADRIAN: You mean?

SIMON: Yeah.

ADRIAN: Well, I suppose, I mean. I just never thought you'd want /

SIMON: Something to discuss.

ADRIAN: Yes. Something to discuss.

SIMON: Something else to discuss.

ADRIAN giggles.

SIMON: What?

ADRIAN: We just take it for granted. All of it. Floating from one day to the next. Trying desperately to shake off that shadow called regret. Running away from it so fast that we never stop to look around us. Forgetting the mistakes we make instead of embracing them and saying, that's fine. What do I need to learn? What's next?

People tell me I overthink things. What's wrong with that? What's the point in living this short life if we don't think about it? And you know what? I've been wrong about so many things. I had grown so used to the idea that I was going to be single forever, you know. Told myself that I'd made my peace with it. I could go out any time, spend money on anything I fancied, and I could sleep on any part of the bed I wanted to. It's fine, I'd say. Relationships, they're for other people. But going out just meant I was that weird guy in the corner of a gay club, alone with a pint, looking like a lost child. I'd waste money on crap I didn't need and, well, I always slept on exactly the same side of the bed every night. Too scared to stretch out a leg because the coldness of the sheet just emphatically reminded me that it was empty. You saved me from that. I didn't think I needed just anyone. That bit turned out to be true. I didn't need just anyone. I just needed you.

SIMON places his head on ADRIAN'S shoulder.

And there's one more thing I am so wrong about. Because you're right, we've lost too many people, and now can't tell them how we feel. Too many people we will never get the chance to. So, here goes.

ADRIAN stands up.

SIMON: No! You're not going to /

ADRIAN: I bloody well am. Simon Collins, I fuckin' love you.

SIMON laughs out loud.

SIMON: Well just as well. Because I fuckin' love you too.

They kiss. The final verses of 'Under Pressure' play.

THE END